# AIN'T NO SUNSHINE

*Leslie DuBois*

# AIN'T NO SUNSHINE

# LESLIE DUBOIS

LITTLE PRINCE PUBLISHING

Published by Little Prince Publishing in Charleston, South Carolina.
Cover Design: Sybil Nelson
Cover Photo: istockphoto

.

ISBN-13: 978-1453772645 (CreateSpace)
ISBN-10: 1453772642

Printed in the United States of America
Visit www.LittlePrincePublishing.com

*Dedicated to Michael*

# Prologue

The officer placed a cup of black coffee on the table in front of me.

"I don't drink coffee," I said, continuing to stare out the window at the Chicago skyline.

"Well, you might want to start. You're not going anywhere for a while, son."

I crossed my arms and slouched in the chair. "I'm not your son," I said through gritted teeth. I focused on a pale yellow Volkswagen van driving past the window of the police station. I shook my head with frustrated regret. I should have bought a new car before we left. I never thought a broken taillight, of all things, would land us in this police station. Now they were asking me questions. Questions I wasn't prepared to answer. Not yet, anyway.

The officer didn't respond at first. The only sound was that of the rotating fan in the corner of the room, blowing out the same hot, stale air.

"Fine," he said after a few minutes. "Let's talk about whose son you are then, huh?" He took some pictures out of a file and laid them out on the table. I refused to look; I knew what they would show. "Do you see this, Stephen? Why don't you look at your father's mutilated body? Beaten to death with a shovel outside his own home."

He picked up one of the pictures and waved it in front of my face. I shut my eyes tightly. I was there when it happened. I knew what it looked like. I didn't want to be reminded of the image; it was already permanently ingrained in my mind.

"Did you do it, Stephen? Did you kill your own father in cold blood?"

I kept my eyes closed and refused to answer. The image of my father's bloody corpse floated behind my eyelids.

"No, you couldn't have done it." I heard the officer's footsteps as he walked to the other side of the room. "There's no way a smart, wealthy boy like you could murder the man that took care of you and loved you for eighteen years."

I opened my eyes and glared at the fat, sweaty man interrogating me. "My father never loved me. Never!"

His eyes expanded. My tone shocked him. He took a step back as if he was actually afraid of me for a second. He quickly recovered his composure, though. "Well, then I guess you *did* kill him."

I bit my tongue and turned away. I had already said too much. There was no way he was getting me to talk. Not yet, anyway. I needed a few more minutes to get my thoughts together.

"I guess we're gonna have to do this the hard way," he said after a few moments. He sat down in the chair across from me and opened his file again. "Maybe I'll just have to ask that pretty little colored girlfriend of yours," he said, staring at Ruthie's picture and licking his lips.

"You leave her out of this." My hands clenched into fists.

"I don't know if I can do that. She seems to be pretty involved." He kept staring at her picture as he spoke. "Your father is found dead at your home in Virginia and you're found seven hundred miles away with a nigger whore. I can't _"

He didn't get to finish his thought. I leapt across the table and started pounding his face in. Seconds later, I was subdued by several officers. They placed me back in the chair and handcuffed me to the table as everyone stepped outside and decided what to do with me.

This was getting worse and worse by the minute. I'd gladly go to jail for killing that man. He deserved to die. I just didn't want Ruthie to get dragged into this. After all we'd been through, at least one of us deserved a chance to be happy.

After what felt like hours, another officer entered the room. He placed a bottle of peroxide and some napkins on the table.

"You gonna behave?" he asked, holding up the key to the handcuffs. He was much younger than the other officer. With his dark hair and blue eyes he kind of reminded me of my older brother, Matthew, except with a bushy mustache. For some reason, I felt I could trust him.

I nodded and he unlocked my handcuffs.

"What's that for?" I asked, indicating the peroxide.

He looked at me strangely. "Stephen, your face is covered in cuts and bruises. The officers who subdued you kind of went a little too far. You have open wounds. You're bleeding." He pointed to a couple of places on my face. "Doesn't it hurt?"

I shrugged and reached for the bottle and paper towels. I didn't feel pain like most people. It was a coping mechanism I'd developed at an early age.

"I'm Lieutenant Drake," he said, still staring at me as I cleaned my wounds. "This must have been a hard few days for you."

I nodded.

"Your father is dead, your mother is missing, and you and Ruthie are on the run."

I nodded.

"Why are you running? You know running only makes you look guilty, and I don't really believe you killed your father. I don't think you're capable."

I stared at him. "You have no idea what I'm capable of. You have no idea what that man did to me."

"You're right. I don't," he said, trying to hide his surprise at my response. He sat down and crossed his arms. "So why don't you tell me? You obviously have a story and you need someone to listen. So tell me your story. Tell me everything."

# Chapter 1

I don't remember when I met Ruthie. She was just always there. She was the reason I woke up in the morning, the reason I survived as long as I did in my father's house, and the reason he deserved to die.

He did everything he could to keep me away from her. One of my earliest memories was of sitting in the front pew of my father's church and twisting my neck to odd angles in order to get a glimpse of Ruthie in the colored balcony. I remember thinking that whites and coloreds weren't even allowed to worship God together, how were they supposed to be able to fall in love?

On one occasion, when I was about five years old, I turned around for too long. My older brother, Matthew, grabbed my hand as a silent gesture to let me know that I needed to turn back before my father saw. But it was too late. As the choir began their rendition of *Amazing Grace*, I knew no amount of grace would save me from what was coming next.

When we got home, my father sent Matthew to the store. I knew that meant trouble. He always sent Matthew away before he went into a violent tirade. He knew Matthew wouldn't tolerate it. Matthew was sixteen years older than me and proved to be a formidable opponent for my father. Any time my father lifted a hand to me or my mother, Matthew was right there diverting my father's wrath. It always ended up turning into a fierce knock-down-drag-out brawl between the two of them. I think my father began to fear Matthew, thus the new habit of sending him away.

I knew not to tell Matthew what my father did while he was gone; that would just result in a worse beating. I didn't mind that much. It was kind of easier this way. The beating was much shorter and I didn't have to watch my father and brother pound on each other over something that was my fault. I just shouldn't have turned around in church. I needed to learn to control my desire to see Ruthie. The sooner I learned that, the easier both of our lives would be.

"Remove your shirt and lie on the floor," he instructed me.

"Yes, Father." I obeyed, and then watched as he pulled the scourge out of its storage place next to his rifle. It was a special device my father had created that was like a whip with stones in it. He said it was what they used to beat the Christ.

"Do you know what you have done?" he asked, staring at the whip and caressing it like it was an old friend.

14

"Devil in Disguise" by Elvis Presley played on the radio. I tried to focus on the music as my father slowly, methodically laid the whip out on the couch. Then his quiet footsteps followed him over to the radio on top of the television. He switched it off. He didn't like anything covering over the sound of the whip against my skin. I think he enjoyed it.

"Yes, Father," I answered him.

"Never look at the coloreds," he said, glaring at me. I turned away so I wouldn't see the evil gleam in his eye. I buried my face in the shag carpeting, nearly inhaling the fibers. "I'm going to beat those desires out of you."

Tears stung behind my eyes, but not because of the impending torture. His words hurt more. Ruthie was colored. I wasn't supposed to want to be with her. My desires were wrong.

The first blow across my back knocked the wind out of me. I gasped and tried to concentrate on making the room stop spinning. It hurt like hell, but I wasn't allowed to cry. If I cried, he would hit me until I stopped. So I just took it. Even at that young age, I had learned how not to cry or show any emotion at all, for that matter. I was an expert at getting people to see what I wanted them to see.

Maybe he was right. I needed those beatings. I should have used them as a way to purge my impure thoughts about Ruthie. Unfortunately, the pain didn't drive away my thoughts of her. Instead, in an effort to escape my reality, I thought of her more. While my body convulsed in painful spasms, my mind was at peace and in her presence.

During this beating in particular, I tried to plan my next adventure with Ruthie. I was not as creative as she was, so all the things I came up with were boring compared to her ideas. Even if I did come up with something halfway decent to do, by the time Ruthie finished making suggestions to make it better, it never really seemed like my idea anymore. I remember one time I came up with the idea to build a car and drive away from here. Somehow it turned into making a boat, becoming pirates and sailing to Europe. We made a raggedy raft that ended up sinking in the lake, but it was fun trying.

I was so lost in my thoughts I didn't hear Matthew come home.

He tackled my father to the ground. "Leave him alone!" They scrambled around for a while, knocking over anything and everything in their path.

My mother, who had been cowering in the kitchen, came forward and pulled me out of the room. "Go to Ruthie's house, Stephen," she said. She looked sad and helpless. Her once-beautiful blue eyes had lost their luster. She probably should have come with me. There was nothing she could do here. They would keep fighting until one of them was out cold. Hopefully, my father would go out first. That would give my mother enough time to get the house cleaned up. If he came to and things looked slightly normal he was able to pretend that nothing had happened and that he didn't just get beat by a boy half his age. My mother and Matthew wouldn't dream of calling  the police or anything. No one would believe that Reverend Phillips would do such a thing, and Matthew would probably be the one taken away. No, we were all just trapped, doomed to continue this cycle over and over again. Deep down I knew it couldn't go on forever. I knew one of them would eventually kill the other. I just didn't know how soon that would happen and how it would affect the rest of my life.

# Chapter 2

We lived in a huge, white, colonial-style house situated in a wooded area on a hill. It had been passed down through my father's family for generations. For a long time, tourists would come to our house as they went through tours of Civil War trails. My father had put an end to that some years ago, though. It would be too embarrassing for him if someone witnessed how he treated us. My father liked this house because he was able to look down on the rest of the town, and, of course, because from here no one could hear our screams.

The only house within walking distance was Ruthie's. Hers was a cottage located at the edge of our property that used to be for servants. It was small, but I liked it much better than my own. It was cozy. Plus, I didn't have to fear for my life when I was there.

As I walked to Ruthie's house, sweat dripped into the open wounds on my back. I must have grimaced with pain because as soon as Ruthie saw me, her eyes saddened and her lips quivered. She knew what had happened. She automatically ran into her house to get the peroxide. By the time I reached her front porch she was ready to doctor my wounds.

"That bastard," she mumbled as she gently cleaned my back. I don't even think she knew what that word meant. It was just something she had heard someone say.

"It's not so bad this time. Matthew was there."

It *wasn't* so bad that time. I had been through much worse. Sometimes I would pass out during his attacks and wake up convulsing in Matthew's arms. For a while, I would have flashbacks whenever a word or smell reminded me of my father. I would freeze at the slightest stimulus. But over time I learned to deal with it. I trained myself to get over those episodes. I had to learn how to not let my father's behavior haunt me in other aspects of my life. That day I was actually able to forget about it and salvage the rest of the afternoon with my friend. I wanted to go swimming in the lake between our houses, but Ruthie thought my back might get infected so she talked me out of it. Instead, we played hide and seek. I ended up staying for dinner that night.

"Mabel, you and your friend get in here for supper," her grandmother yelled into the woods from the kitchen window. Mabel was Ruthie's mother. I don't know how she got them confused. From the pictures I saw, they looked nothing alike. Mabel had a smooth, dark complexion with thick, black hair. She had big, round eyes and a round face. Ruthie's eyes were more almond-shaped, and everyone called her "high yellow." We know now that they were referring to her light complexion, but back then those comments just started Ruthie's love affair with the color yellow.

"Grandma, I'm not Mabel. I'm Ruthie. Mabel was my mommy, and she died a long time ago."

"Don't you think I know that?" Grandma Esther said. She really didn't know. She was just too proud to ever admit she was wrong. "And who is your friend?"

"Grandma this is Stephen Phillips. He's been here all day." Ruthie rested her head on her little fist. I could tell she was getting upset at the mention of her mother. It made her sad to think that she had never met her. Ruthie's mother died in childbirth.

Grandma Esther asked who I was so often that sometimes we would make it a game and tell her I was some television star she had never heard of. One time we even told her I was President Kennedy's son, and she gave us an extra dessert at dinner. I guess Ruthie didn't feel like playing that game today.

"You must be Theodore's boy." For a long time, I had no idea who she was talking about. I thought Theodore was some white person she had met when she was young and thus she naturally thought I was related to him. I was ten when I first learned that Theodore was my father's first name.

21

Late that night, Matthew came over to collect me. Ruthie and I had fallen asleep in front of the television. Ruthie's grandmother had forgotten to lock the front door, as usual, so Matthew just came in. He picked me up and was about to walk out when Ruthie woke up.

"Wait, Matthew. It's your gift day." She rubbed the sleep from her eyes. Her dark brown curls were in a tangled mass on one side of her head. In the summer, the sun always dyed a few select strands of hair a light gold color, which made it look like she had yellow ribbons in her hair. She jumped up and scurried to her bedroom. Matthew set me down on the sofa and looked at me for an explanation, but I just shrugged. I had no idea what she was talking about. I was with her all day and I didn't see her making any gifts. This must have been something she had planned earlier.

Ruthie came into the living room, smiling broadly and with her hands behind her back.

"Close your eyes," she told Matthew. I could tell that he was exhausted but he played along and tried to perk up.

"What's this about, kiddo? What do you mean it's my 'gift day'?" he asked playfully.

Ruthie liked to choose random days, give them a name, and hand out gifts. She always thought it was sad that people only gave each other gifts on birthdays and Christmas. I think the real reason was that her birthday marked the death of her mother. And her senile grandmother never remembered Christmas.

"I mean you get a gift today because it's a very special day." Ruthie cleared her throat and tried to sound official and grown up. "This is August of 1963. August is the ninth month of the year. Nine plus sixty-three is seventy-two. Seventy-two minus fifty is twenty-two which makes this a very special day because fifty days from today you will be twenty-two years old." Ruthie was so proud of her convoluted logic that she almost forgot to give Matthew his surprise.

"Oh, here you go," she said as she handed him a very elaborate picture colored with a combination of crayons and finger paint. "You can open your eyes now."

Matthew had been smiling throughout Ruthie's speech, but when he saw the picture his smile waned. He looked sad. Ruthie started to get upset.

"You don't like it?" she asked, on the verge of tears. "I can make you another one."

"No, Ruthie, I love it. It's perfect," he choked. I didn't really understand why he got so emotional back then.

"You see, it's us," Ruthie began to explain with renewed vigor. "There's Stephen and there's me. See how my skin is darker. And there's you and Miss Marjorie. I didn't have any more yellow so I made her hair brown. Is that okay? I know what you're thinking. That the sun is very yellow and I could have used some of that yellow on Miss Marjorie's hair, but the sun isn't yellow. It's a new color I found called saffron. Isn't that a pretty name for a color?"

Ruthie kept going on about the drawing, pointing out the lake and the tire swing and how the sun took up nearly half the picture. That was her way of showing that everyone was happy. She even had her grandmother in the picture. Everything and everyone was there--except my father.

Even though Matthew was exhausted and probably in a lot of pain, he still carried me all the way home. I felt guilty and offered to walk, but I think he preferred to hold me. He walked in silence. I tried to figure out why he was so sad. Maybe Ruthie's picture reminded him of the kind of life he wanted. He was old enough to leave and start a family of his own, but he didn't. Maybe it showed him a glimpse of what life could be like if a certain someone wasn't around. We didn't have any family pictures like that where everyone seemed happy. As a matter of fact, we didn't have any family pictures with Matthew in them. Now that I think of it, I don't remember seeing a single childhood photo of Matthew. It was like he wasn't a part of this family or like someone was purposely trying to exclude him.

# Chapter 3

When we got home, my mother was on the sofa crying. Matthew tucked me into bed and then went to console her. He held her in his arms and let her sob uncontrollably. She would be there for hours, then she would fall asleep and he would carry her to bed.

That night I had a dream. It wasn't anything elaborate or symbolic. It was so simple and calming, yet memorable at the same time. Ruthie and I were walking down Main Street of Livingston, Virginia hand in hand. That's all. Just walking down the street. Yet, as simple as that sounded, it wasn't possible. We'd tried it before. Last winter we were waiting for Matthew outside of a whites-only pharmacy when I noticed Ruthie was cold. I grabbed her hands to warm them in mine. The store owner came out and yelled at us. Matthew swept us up, tossed us in the car and drove away as fast as he could. My father already knew what happened by the time we got home. The next day, when Matthew went to work, he beat me.

The Wednesday after I messed up and got caught looking at Ruthie during church, Ruthie and I sat in her living room watching TV. There was a man on television talking about a dream he'd had. I remember thinking that his dream was much better than mine. Ruthie was glued to the television as Martin Luther King talked about how "little black boys and little black girls will be able to join hands with little white boys and little white girls as sisters and brothers."

"That's us," Ruthie said with tears in her eyes as she grabbed my hand. "He's talking about us."

\*\*\*

Normally, it is the mother who takes her children shopping, but not in my family. My father never let my mother leave the house except for church and a few very important social functions where it would look bad if she didn't attend. He treated her like some sort of caged animal, controlling her every move. Watching my mother cook a meal was like watching a puppeteer with a marionette. He would sit in the kitchen and stare at her. He only allowed her to use certain ingredients and utensils. If she added too many dashes of salt or used a spoon he had never seen before, he made her throw the food away and start over.

With school starting in a few days, I needed new clothes. God forbid I not look like the perfect child he had groomed me to be. My father and I went to the local department stores while Matthew stayed at home with mother. Matthew knew he wouldn't do anything to me with people watching. I actually didn't mind going shopping with my father. He was nice to me in public. He played the role of loving father so well that even I almost believed it. We would wander around the store together and he would let me pick out what I wanted. After rejecting half of the items as inappropriate, I would then go try on the rest of the clothes to see if they met his approval. Each item had to be of a certain quality and reflect the amount of money my father had.

Our shopping trips never lasted too long, but they were a great escape for me. This time, before we went to pay for everything, my father did something very odd. He went over to the ladies' section and started looking around. I thought he was going to buy something for my mother until he picked up a little yellow dress. I was completely confused.

"Will this fit Ruthie?" I don't remember if I answered him or not, but it didn't matter. He was so fixated on the dress he wouldn't have heard me anyway. "Yellow is her favorite color isn't it?" he asked. This I knew for sure. She was always running out of yellow crayons. If she could she would color everything yellow. She had even somehow managed to get her cottage painted yellow. I nodded yes as we walked toward the register. Why was he buying a dress for Ruthie?

"Hello, Reverend Phillips. How are you today?" the cashier asked.

"I'm doing just fine, praise be to the Lord."

"Oh, is this for a niece of yours?" she asked when she came to the little yellow dress. I wondered if my father would lie to save face, but he didn't.

"No, it's for a little Negro girl that lives near my house." The cashier looked almost disgusted as if the dress was suddenly tainted. "As you know," he added, "I have just opened the doors of my church to the Negro community." By "opening his doors" he meant allowing them to sit in the balcony, which was even hotter than where we sat. But I guess that was more than what other churches were doing. "I think all people should have a chance to repent of their sins and be blessed with God's glory, don't you?"

The cashier nodded guiltily in agreement.

"I'm just trying to make sure that when they come before the Lord, they look somewhat presentable. And if I have to do that one little child at a time, I will."

"You're such a kind-hearted man, Reverend. God bless you." It made me sick the way people fawned over him like he was heaven incarnate. He fooled everyone into thinking he was just simply angelic. In public, his light brown eyes would glisten and gleam with kindness and sincerity, but at home I was sure those eyes were from Satan himself. He did things like this once in a while just to

28

convince people of his goodness. Ruthie wouldn't be fooled. She knew the truth about him. She would reject the dress. I knew she would.

"Thank you, young lady." My father tipped his hat and kissed the cashier's hand. She grinned like an idiot while she put all of our purchases in a bag.

On the way home, we stopped at Ruthie's house. He wanted me to wait in the car, but I got out anyway when he wasn't looking.

"No, thank you, sir. I don't need another dress," I heard her say. I knew she wouldn't take it. My father had a strange look on his face. No one ever told him no except Matthew, and that always led to a fight. Suddenly, I got afraid. What if he tried to hurt her? But he didn't get angry.

"How about I make you a deal? Just try it on. If it fits and you like it, you don't have to take it off." Ruthie stared at the dress. It was too much of a temptation. It was a pretty dress, I guess, covered with lace and bows and all that frilly stuff girls like. And it was in her absolute favorite color. She couldn't resist.

"Okay," she conceded as she started to walk to her room to try it on. He grabbed her little hand. Ruthie was always very little for her age. I think it came from her being born two months premature.

"You can change here. It's okay," he said. Why did he want her to change in front of him? I started to feel sick.

I didn't know what all of this meant, but I didn't like it. Something wasn't right.

# Chapter 4

Months went by without any more run-ins between Matthew and my father. Life felt kind of normal except for the occasional strange episodes between my father and Ruthie. I remember him saying he was trying to help the entire Negro Community, but I only saw him buying things for her.

That fall Ruthie and I went back to school. We were going to Kindergarten. It was the first time we would be going to the same school. Our town was far behind the rest of the nation when it came to matters of integration. That was partly due to the prejudices of old rich racists and partly due to the fact that there was just not a lot of diversity in our town. We didn't even have a colored school. The few colored kids were bused an hour and a half away to the nearest integrated school. Last year, instead of making that bus trip, my mother taught Ruthie at home. I loved to play sick sometimes so I could stay home with them.

"Did you know my mommy, Miss Marjorie?" Ruthie asked my mother one day during her reading lesson. I had stayed home that day with a "stomachache."

"I did. She was my best friend," my mother said. I had never heard her talk about Mabel before. It hadn't even occurred to me that they might have been friends.

"Did it make you sad when she died?"

"I was very sad, Ruthie." My mother started tearing up.

"Don't cry, Miss Marjorie," Ruthie said as she hugged her. "I get sad when I think about her sometimes, too. But, we still have each other." My mother smiled weakly and returned the embrace. She regained her composure and tried to continue with the reading lesson, but Ruthie's curiosity had not yet been satisfied.

"Did you know my daddy?"

"Yes, I did," my mother answered suddenly turning cold.

"What was he like?" My mother closed the book and looked Ruthie directly in the eyes.

"He loved your mother very much. But he's gone and he's never coming back. Don't think about him."

"If he loved her, why did he leave her? Why did he leave me?" My mother couldn't answer those questions. How was she supposed to know what was going through the mind of Ruthie's father? Ruthie would have to be satisfied just knowing that she was a product of love. That was more than I could say for myself.

Now that we were in the same school, I got to see Ruthie even more often. In the mornings, she would come over right after her bath, and my mother would dress her and fix her hair. After breakfast, we would hop in the car, and Matthew would drive us to school. We could've taken the bus, but I think Matthew enjoyed spending time with us. In school, we were in different classes. I thought it was because they thought Ruthie wouldn't be prepared since she didn't go to preschool, but it was really that they still wanted to keep the Negro kids separate from the white. They were all shocked when she surpassed everyone in her class due to the education my mother had given her.

I always wished we were in the same classes, but it still made me happy to know that she was only a few doors away. Sometimes I would collect all the yellow crayons in my classroom, tie them together with a bow like a bouquet, and take them down to her classroom as a gift. I knew she would be running out frequently.

My mother had prepared Ruthie academically, but I don't think she was ready for school, socially. She had only been around her grandmother, me, and my family and she wasn't aware of how nasty other people could be, especially children.

"Why don't you go back to the jungle, monkey," Paul Morrison said to Ruthie before spitting in her hair. Then he pushed her down before running out to the playground.

Ruthie didn't jump up and retaliate like most kindergartners would. Instead she calmly stood up, closed her eyes and smiled. She was able to look inside herself and find a happy thought to get her through. I hoped that happy thought was about me.

I wasn't as forgiving as Ruthie, however. I ran outside and found Paul about to board the merry-go-round. I tackled him and started pounding his face into the dirt.

"Stephen, stop it," I heard Ruthie say seconds later. "He doesn't matter. Stop, Stephen, stop."

Out of the corner of my eye, I saw Ruthie crying. She was crying because of me. I didn't want to cause her any more pain, so I stopped punching Paul and started to get off of him. That's when he hit me with a sucker punch to my left eye before running away.

"Why did you do that?" Ruthie asked, holding ice to my eye. Kids pointed and shook their heads as they walked past us sitting outside the cafeteria.

"He shouldn't have done that to you."

Ruthie shook her head. "Now they're going to pick on you, too. You get picked on enough at home."

The white kids at school did call me names for a few weeks, but it didn't last. They soon forgot about me and just went back to tormenting Ruthie. Unfortunately, she didn't even get relief from people of her own race. The colored kids teased her because she was too light-skinned.

\*\*\*

Matthew picked us up every day from school. Fridays were special days. Instead of going straight home, we would walk around and look at the scenery of our quaint little town. Horse-drawn carriages looked more appropriate on the street than cars did. Sometimes we went to the park to play, but we always stopped at the ice cream shop on Main Street. Ruthie and I would wait outside while Matthew went in and bought us a sundae to share between the three of us. I don't remember there being a "whites only" sign, but it must have been implied since Ruthie never went in. One Friday after ice cream, we didn't take the normal way home.

"Where are we going?" I remember asking.

"I have a surprise for you. Both of you," he said as he tousled Ruthie's already messy hair. My mother always fixed her hair into two neat and adorably curly pigtails in the morning, and by lunch it always resembled a desert tumbleweed. She was also notorious for getting paint and markers in her hair. My mother gave up asking her how it got there; Ruthie never remembered.

Matthew's surprise for us was a Golden Retriever that he had bought from the pet store. Ruthie was so excited that she squealed and danced around it and scared the puppy so much that he wet on her, but she didn't care. We spent the entire trip home arguing over what to name her.

"I think we should call her Yellowbird," Ruthie said.

"But she's not yellow; she's more of a gold color," I said. "And she's not a bird." Matthew laughed. I was always very literal even as a child.

"She doesn't have to be a bird to be called Yellowbird, Stephen. And gold is a type of yellow," she said, annoyed that I was taking the fun out of the naming process.

"She's got a point there, Stephen." Matthew cleared his throat and tried to sound serious.

"Why don't we name her Goldie?" I said.

"That's not creative at all. Where's your imagination, Stephen? I'm calling her Yellowbird."

"Well, I'm calling her Goldie." We never did decide what the official name of the dog was.

One weekend a couple of months after school started my father went out of town. Matthew thought it was a perfect occasion to try to make Ruthie's picture come true. He organized a picnic by the lake. It wasn't exactly like the picture; the sun wasn't a bright saffron color, Ruthie's grandmother didn't come because she felt ill, it was chilly and nearly all the leaves had fallen off the trees, but it was still my best childhood memory. My mother actually smiled and laughed as Matthew playfully chased her through the trees. When night came, Matthew made a fire and we all snuggled around it together. I didn't want it to end. But it did.

That night while I was sleeping, my father came home. He and Matthew started fighting, but somehow it felt different. It was worse. I heard terrified shrieks from my mother and what sounded like furniture being thrown against the walls. Suddenly, Matthew burst into my room and told me to go to Ruthie's house. When I didn't move fast enough he picked me up, put a blanket around me, and carried me to the back door. Then my mother screamed the most gut-wrenching scream I had ever heard. I turned to see what was going on, but Matthew pushed me out of the door. All I saw was my father dragging my mother by her hair with one hand and waving his rifle with the other. Matthew tried to wrestle the gun away from him. When I heard a shot fire, I ran away as fast as my feet would carry me to Ruthie's cottage.

I stayed at Ruthie's house for three days waiting for Matthew. I hoped he'd won the battle, but when my mother, not Matthew, finally came to get me, I knew otherwise. She looked horrible. My father had never beaten her so badly before. She wouldn't be able to go out in public for weeks.

"Where's Matthew?" I asked.

My mother stared straight ahead and said, "He's gone."

# Chapter 5

"So your dad killed your older brother?" the lieutenant asked. He took a deep breath and let it out slowly as if trying to process the information. "Is that why you killed him?"

I didn't respond. I couldn't.

"Was it self-defense?" he added.

I looked out of the window and fought back tears of anger. I wouldn't cry. I refused.

"Stephen, I want to help you. But you have to work with me. You have to tell me the truth."

I shrugged. "What is truth anyway? What does it matter?"

"The truth is everything. The truth shall set you free."

I turned and glared at him then. My father often quoted that scripture in his sermons. I hated those words. They were empty and meaningless coming from my father and they certainly weren't going to help me get out of my current situation. If anything, the so-called truth had ruined my life.

"I will never be free," I said, turning away from him again.

"Is that because you're lying to me?"

I do lie sometimes. Everyone does. But not dangerous lies. I lie to protect people.

Lieutenant Drake stood and walked to the window. "Smoke?" he asked holding out a cigarette for me.

I shook my head. "I'm allergic."

Lieutenant Drake looked at the cigarette then put it back in the pack, choosing not to send me into an allergic reaction.

"In eighth grade, Ruthie and I decided to experiment with cigarettes. We met behind the gymnasium and held the cigarettes between our fingers for ten minutes before we had the courage to actually light them."

"What happened?"

"It took about three seconds before my throat closed up and I couldn't breathe. Ruthie ran to get the school nurse. After the principal and the nurse were sure I wasn't going to die, Ruthie and I faced suspension for smoking on school property. But I told them it wasn't her. I was alone and she just happened to be walking past to find me choking."

"You protected her."

I nodded. "It was the least I could do. I owe her. Without her in my life..." I couldn't finish the thought. I didn't know what my life would be like without Ruthie. I probably would've killed myself by the time I was ten.

"What did your dad do when he found out you got suspended?"

"I didn't get suspended."

Lieutenant Drake looked a question at me.

"Why not?"

"My father called the principal. Worked his magic. Got the suspension revoked. But when I got home -"

"He beat you." Lieutenant Drake said, finishing my thought.

"He broke my collarbone." I self-consciously touched the slight bump where the bone hadn't healed properly.

Lieutenant Drake sighed, then sat back down.

"I don't know why I'm telling you this," I said. "I guess I feel if you know me, you'll understand me. No one understands me except Ruthie."

Lieutenant Drake leaned back in his chair. "Why don't you tell me more about her? How did she deal with Matthew's death?"

# Chapter 6

The next few weeks were miserable. My father tortured my mother. He kicked her in the stomach, pushed her down stairs, and beat her to within an inch of her life. He told the congregation that she had gone to California to visit her family so no one would get suspicious.

I worried about her. She would go days at a time without eating. My father wouldn't let her. I would sneak into her room and try to give her some food. Sometimes he would catch me and beat me, too. One morning, he left to run some errands. I called Ruthie and had her bring over some of her grandmother's biscuits. I tried to feed Mother, but she was in so much pain it hurt for her to even sit up.

"I'm sorry, Stephen," she said weakly.

"Shh, just try to eat something, Mother." I didn't know why she tried to apologize to me. She didn't do anything wrong. She swallowed a couple of bites of food and almost vomited.

"It's all my fault. I'm so sorry, Stephen." She was delirious. She didn't know what she was talking about. My father had driven her crazy. I tried to quiet her down.

"Don't try to talk. Just eat."

"Just remember I love you. No matter what happens, I love you. I did it for you." Her tone frightened me. She sounded like she was giving up. What did she mean, she did it for me? What did she do? She started convulsing and vomiting blood. I thought she was going to die right there in front of my eyes. But she didn't. She survived.

Whenever someone asked, my father claimed Matthew ran away to join the Navy. I knew that wasn't true. I was convinced that he killed my brother and hid the body. I also knew Ruthie was devastated, but she didn't want to let it show. She tried to be strong. I remember she dragged me to the police station in order to file an official complaint against my father.

"I wanna report a murder," she said as she marched into the Livingston police station. It was a little country station with only two or three officers comprising the entire force. The building was smaller than my house. At first, no one even acknowledged our presence. Ruthie had to repeat herself three times before anyone even looked at her.

"What kind of a murder would you like to report, little girl?" Stanley Pender asked as he knelt down, smiling at Ruthie. At the time, I thought he was about 150 years old. I probably wasn't too far off. He was a relic at the police station. I think he was the first officer in the town. These days he never did any real work. He was more of an honorary deputy. "Is it your dog? Did someone hurt your dog?" he added.

"No," Ruthie said still determined, "someone killed my Matthew. His brother," she added, pointing to me. I had stayed a few steps behind her with my head down. I was a little embarrassed. I knew no one would believe her. They would give her the same look my pre-school teacher had given me when I tried to tell her what my father did to me and my mother.

"And just who killed Matthew?" he asked, still smiling.

"Reverend Phillips," Ruthie stated boldly. Stanley's smile melted off his face.

"Girl, you can't go 'round accusin' innocent people of thangs. Do you know what God does to liars?"

"The same thing he does to murderers! Thankfully, I don't have to worry about that. I ain't a liar!" Ruthie yelled with her hands on her hips. "He did it. I know he did!"

"Stephen," Stanley called still staring at Ruthie. I thought he might take off his belt and give her a beating right there.

"Yes, Sir."

"Why don't you go home and teach your colored friend some manners? And tell her your brother joined the Navy. He's not dead."

"Yes, Sir." I grabbed Ruthie's hand and tried to pull her out of the station. She kept ranting about how my father was a murderer and how we might be next.

"He wouldn't leave without saying goodbye! He's dead, I know it!" No one listened.

Ruthie and I sat on the stone steps outside the police station as the skies darkened. We sat there in silence for what seemed like forever. I knew Ruthie was trying to come up with a plan. I thought she'd want to leave as I felt the first few drops of rain. Grandma Esther had just straightened her hair and any kind of moisture would make it curl up again. But Ruthie didn't move. She just sat there. As the rain started to come down harder, Ruthie started to cry. Matthew had been like a father to her. He was another one to add to the list of people she loved that had left her.

We coped with our grief by searching for Matthew's body in the woods. Ruthie thought that if we found a body maybe someone would believe us. We let Goldie sniff his clothes and run around the woods, thinking she could find where my father had buried Matthew. She was just a puppy, though, and most of the time she'd end up chasing a squirrel while Ruthie and I continued the search. We looked for clues and even dug numerous holes, thinking we had found his grave. We finally decided that we would never find his body and gave ourselves some closure by holding a memorial service for him by the lake.

We both dressed in black and met at the lake right before sunset. Ruthie drew a picture of Matthew, and we taped it to a tree during the service. Then we both gave speeches, sharing what we loved about Matthew and what we would miss the most.

"I'm gonna miss the way he'd tuck me in at night and tell me that everything was gonna be okay and the way he made me feel safe," I said.

As tears trickled down her face, Ruthie said "I'm gonna miss the way he would put me on his shoulders on the way to the park and how he would pick us up from school every day and on Fridays take us for ice cream."

Then Ruthie sang "You Are My Sunshine" because that was her favorite song to sing with Matthew. I felt the song was pretty appropriate. For our entire lives, Matthew was the only ray of sunshine. Next, we took the drawing of Matthew and buried it in one of the holes we had dug, looking for his grave.

My life got much worse without Matthew. My mother became just a shell of her former self. She barely spoke, even to me. Sometimes she would just look at me and start crying. Then she would grab me and say "I'm sorry" over and over again. I guess she was apologizing for the way my father treated us. She thought it was her fault that she didn't have the strength to take me and leave. I didn't blame her, though.  I could handle the abuse.  I had gotten used to it. It was just mind over matter for me.

# Chapter 7

Every day during the summer, Ruthie and I went swimming in our lake. One day, when I was thirteen, our innocent summer recreation became something more.

I was sitting on the grass, taking a break, when she sauntered out of the water. Suddenly, I saw her differently. She wasn't a little girl anymore. She was still my best friend on the inside, but on the outside she had changed. I finally noticed she was absolutely gorgeous.

"Are you coming back in the water?" she asked, completely unaware that I was undressing her with my eyes. It wasn't difficult to do, considering the tiny yellow swimsuit she wore. We were so close that we often overlooked modesty with each other. At that moment, I mentally thanked whoever had created the bikini.

"Stephen? Are you okay?" I realized that I had missed her question because I was too busy staring at her breasts. A flush came over me, and I felt a warm sensation all over my body, especially in my swim trunks.

"Stephen, why are you all red? Are you sick?" She went to touch my face.

"No, don't touch me." I jerked away from her hand.

"What's wrong? Did I do something?" She was starting to worry.

"No...uh...yeah, I'm sick. I just don't want you to catch it. I think I better go home." I went to stand up but realized that something was going on in my pants. I sat back down and put a towel over my lap. Oh my God, I had an erection. How could just looking at Ruthie evoke such a response? My face reddened even more at the thought of how badly I wanted her to touch me...to touch it.

"I thought you were leaving," she said, looking at me like I was crazy.

"I am. I will…in a minute. I...I think I want to watch the lake for a while, first," I lied. All I wanted to watch was her and her soft, caramel skin. Her sopping-wet hair hung down to the middle of her back, touching the little latch that kept her bathing suit top on. I wanted that latch to break so badly. I thought that maybe if I stared at it long enough it would, but it didn't. Ruthie finally got tired of trying to figure out what was wrong with me.

"Well, I'm going home. Feel better, okay?" She stood and walked away from me. I watched as a single drop of water rolled down her back and over the swell of her butt. It was the luckiest drop of water I had ever seen in my life.

50

That day, I distinctly remember missing Matthew more than usual. Not a day went by that I didn't think about him or wonder what he would look like at a certain age. Sometimes I would momentarily forget the sound of his voice or what he was like. I'd try to talk about him to my mother, but she would usually just start crying and leave the room.

I knew if Matthew were there, I'd be able to talk to him about what I was feeling for Ruthie. Without Matthew, I had no one. I had no one to tell me how to make it stop.

Usually, I told Ruthie all my problems. We didn't have any secrets between us. But how could I tell her this? How do you tell your best friend that you are sexually attracted to her? I had just decided that this was one thing I would keep to myself when I heard a knock on my door. It was Ruthie. She hated coming to my house. My father made her feel uncomfortable, but she always made the sacrifice if I was sick or if she thought I needed her.

"Are you still not feeling good? I brought you some soup." She stepped into my room. "I made it myself. Do you want to try some? It's normal, I promise." Ruthie was not the best cook. She was much too creative. When Ruthie cooked, by the time she finished adding garnish and trying to make the food look pretty, it was pretty much unrecognizable and inedible. I was quite often forced to be the taste tester. I would try to be positive, but she always knew when I was

51

lying. Once in a while she did create something truly delicious, but those times were few and far between. Her failures in the kitchen never discouraged her from trying again, though. She always said that one success was worth a thousand failures. My stomach disagreed.

"Um...no...I mean yes...um." I felt like an idiot. I couldn't even formulate a complete sentence around her anymore. I had to get control of myself.

"Huh?"

"No, I am not still sick and yes, I would like to try some of your soup."

"Good." Ruthie plopped down on my bed and handed me the bowl and a spoon. The thought of her next to me on my bed made me excited again. I closed my eyes and tried to get a hold of myself.

"Stephen, what's wrong? Why are you acting so strange?"

I opened my eyes, but when I looked at her, sitting on my bed, so close to me that I could feel her warmth, I had to turn away.

Ruthie grabbed my chin and gently turned my face toward her. She stared deep in my eyes like she was trying to read my soul. Her striking, light brown eyes were so beautiful. They were the type of eyes that you could spot from across the room. She took her little hand and wiped away the beads of sweat that were beginning to form above my brow. She smelled so good. When had she started wearing perfume? Or maybe it wasn't perfume. Maybe she just naturally smelled like flowers. Suddenly, I had the urge to kiss her. My lips tingled with anticipation. I think she finally figured out what I was thinking. Her eyes expanded to twice their size.

"I gotta go." She quickly jumped off my bed, nearly tipping over the soup in my hands.

"Don't go," I pleaded. Now I had done it. I had scared her away. What if she didn't feel the same way? I'm such an idiot, I thought. Ruthie stopped in the doorway and smiled at me.

"I'll see you tomorrow, Stephen," she said as she bounced out the door. I knew we would be okay.

I wasn't the only one to notice how Ruthie had changed nearly overnight. Whenever she was around, my father couldn't take his eyes off of her.

"Ruth, come sit with me for a moment," he said to her as she was trying to sneak out of my house unnoticed.

"I really can't, sir. I have to get back to my grandmother. She's not feeling well."

"I'm sorry to hear that. She will be in my prayers. Is there anything I can do?"

"No, we're fine. I just need to get back."

"Why don't you sit and talk to me for a while and then I'll give you a ride back. I'll even take you into town and we can pick up some groceries." Ruthie wanted to protest, but he grabbed her hands and led her to the sofa. He sat next to her and started stroking her hair.

"What did you and Stephen do today?" he asked.

"We went swimming in the lake, but Stephen got sick and came home," Ruthie replied. She was so tense and nervous; she looked like she wanted to cry.

"That's nice." He wasn't even listening to her. "You are a beautiful child. Do you know that?" I couldn't take it anymore. I came into the living room as loudly as possible.

"Ruthie, you're still here. Um...isn't it your turn to walk Goldie?" I couldn't think of anything else to say.

"Oh, I forgot. Come here, Yellowbird." Recognizing a way out, she bolted off the sofa. "Excuse me, Reverend Phillips."

My father stared after her. Then he put his face in his hands...and cried.

# Chapter 8

Ruthie and I got a lot closer that summer. Our hugs became longer and more meaningful, and we would hold hands when no one was around. We had this unstated commitment to each other. Once, my father caught us watching TV together. We weren't doing anything wrong. I don't even think we were touching, but he could sense that there was something between us and he didn't like it. Maybe it was the way she smiled at me or the way I would move the loose strands of hair out of her face when they got in the way.

"Ruth, please leave," he said. Ruthie could tell from his tone of voice that he meant business. She was practically off the sofa before he finished the sentence.

"What's going on between you two?"

"Nothing, Father; we're just friends. She's my best friend." She's my only friend, I thought.

"It better stay that way. Anything else would be inappropriate and I will not allow that. Do you understand?" When I didn't answer right away he grabbed my neck forcefully and squeezed.

"I said, 'do you understand?'" He had such a tight grip on me that I nearly passed out.

"Yes, I understand." But I really didn't understand. I couldn't quite tell if he was angry because I was getting close to a colored person or if he was angry because I was getting close to Ruthie. I saw the way he looked at her when he thought I wasn't paying attention. And he continued buying things for her. It was like he was obsessed. If I didn't know any better, I would think *he* was in love with her. But that was absurd. She was just a child in comparison to him. But I had heard of people like that who were obsessed with little children and who abused them. If he ever touched my Ruthie I didn't know what I'd do to him. Maybe I was overreacting. Maybe he just liked Ruthie. She was a likeable girl. As racial barriers had slowly started to melt away, people in town had become more accepting of colored people, especially Ruthie. Everyone loved her. Maybe he liked Ruthie as a person, but just didn't ever want a colored person to be a part of his family. That definitely wouldn't fit the picture-perfect family image that he had worked so hard to create.

Soon after that I went on my first date. Unfortunately, it wasn't with Ruthie. Mary Elizabeth Myers invited me to the Sadie Hawkins dance. She was a pretty blonde girl who attended my father's church. It was probably her parents' dream for their daughter go to a dance with the perfect Stephen Phillips. I bet my father even talked to them and arranged for her to ask me. He was trying to get Ruthie off my mind. "Did you have a good time, tonight?" she asked as we ate ice cream after the dance. We stopped at the same little ice cream shop that Ruthie, Matthew, and I used to frequent on Friday afternoons before he died. I didn't like going there; it reminded me too much of Matthew and made me miss him, but Mary Elizabeth insisted on extending the date. She said they had the 'best chocolate malts' in town. She failed to realize they sold the only chocolate malts in town. Her question was the first time in thirty minutes that she had given me the opportunity to contribute to the conversation; even so, she barely gave me time to respond.

"It was okay." It was *not* okay. The dance was just an excuse for all the rich white parents in town to pair off their children. All the girls wore what looked like the same white dress and all the boys wore tuxedos. When we walked in, we were introduced as "Ms. Mary Elizabeth Myers and her escort, Mr. Stephen Andrew Phillips." It made it seem like I was just one of her accessories. The whole evening felt like a betrothal.

"I thought it was wonderful. They really did an excellent job turning town hall into a formal venue. I mean, did you see all the twinkle lights? It must have taken them hours to do. And the purple lilies were just exquisite. And everyone looked just lovely. Did you see Mary Louise

Roman? Didn't she look great? We were both wearing empire-cut dresses. What are the chances of that? Isn't that funny? And our names are so similar. Did you notice that? She is Mary Louise and I am Mary Elizabeth. I wonder if our parents did that on purpose. They're friends, you know. We could practically be sisters except that I have blonde hair and she has red hair. I usually don't like red hair, but hers is nice. It's a darker red, not that bright, hideous red like Julia Jordan. Ugh, her hair is so disgusting! If Mary Louise's hair ever got that color I would have to insist that she dye it to an appropriate shade. I would *not* be able to tolerate it. Wouldn't that shade of red be just disgusting on someone with Mary Louise's complexion?"

She paused, waiting for me to answer, I guess. I didn't know what to say. I didn't know what hair color would look good with Mary Louise's complexion, nor did I care. Thankfully, she started talking again before I had time to say anything."What a silly question to ask. You're a boy. You don't notice things like that. You probably have no idea about any of that stuff." She wasn't completely right about that. I did notice things like complexion and hair color, just not on people like her, Mary Louise, or Julia. They were vapid morons with whom I had nothing in common. They had no idea what real life was like. They hadn't been forced to face the sadness and pain that Ruthie and I encountered every day. They lived in their own little bubble of polite society, where nothing was ever unpleasant. I think our common suffering is what drew Ruthie and me together. We understood each other and could comfort each other, although I think Ruthie did more for me than I did for her.

While I didn't notice things about most girls, Ruthie was special. I noticed every little thing about her. I noticed that she had a beautiful, soft brown complexion; one like no other. And if the sun hit her at just the right time, she glowed like a golden goddess. And I noticed how her normally dark-brown hair changed to varying shades of light brown, bronze, and blonde depending on how the light hit it. And those eyes, oh my God, those eyes. They were hauntingly beautiful; I saw them in my sleep.

"But you do know when a girl is pretty or not, don't you?" Mary Elizabeth added, interrupting my daydream about Ruthie. She was twisting one of her blonde curls with her finger and tilting her head to the side, trying her best to look cute. "Do you think I'm pretty?" Somehow I had to answer her without giving away that I was really thinking about Ruthie.

"Of course I do," I said as I kissed her hand. I was my normal charming and debonair self. There was a reason I had garnered the reputation of 'that perfect Phillips boy'. And I wasn't lying. I did think she was pretty, in her own way; she was just common and plain compared to Ruthie. My response was enough to send Mary Elizabeth into annoyingly squeaky giggles.  She didn't talk for a good ten minutes and I was able to finish my chocolate malt in peace.

"What are you thinking about?" she asked to break the silence.  I hated that question.  Why did she need to know what I was thinking?  Ruthie never asked me that; she just always seemed to know.  She knew me better than I knew myself.  Mary Elizabeth wanted me to say  that I was thinking about her.  I was tired of playing the game, but I decided to tell her what she wanted to hear, anyway.

After the ice cream shop, she wanted to walk around town with me for a while, but I just wanted to finish the date so I could meet Ruthie.  "A pretty girl like you shouldn't be out at all hours of the night.  You need your beauty rest," I told her.  She giggled and agreed to let me walk her home.  Girls were so easy to manipulate sometimes.

I was relieved to be rid of Mary Elizabeth.  I knew Ruthie would be waiting for me.

"Did you have fun tonight?" she asked before I even had time to sit down.  I could tell she was a little jealous that she didn't get to go with me.  I don't think our little town would have been ready for that.

Ruthie didn't look at me.  She stared at the ground, playing with a few blades of grass as if she was looking for something.  She had on a yellow spring dress without a sweater, even though the temperature was quickly dropping at this time of night.  She probably wore it because she knew

60

it was my favorite. I used to tease her and say it made her look like a dandelion. She was probably freezing, but too stubborn to admit it.

"I guess so," I said as I loosened my cummerbund and bow tie. I hated dressing up. I came very close to throwing the tie and cummerbund into the lake, but that might have resulted in a beating from my father, so I restrained myself. I really didn't want to spend my time with Ruthie talking about Mary Elizabeth, but then it occurred to me that maybe if Ruthie got a little jealous she would finally tell me how she felt about me.

"Did you dance a lot?"

"Yep."

"Did you walk her home?"

"Yeah."

"Hmph." She stopped playing with the grass, crossed her arms and stared out over the lake. She still wouldn't look at me.

"What does that mean?" I asked.

"Well, in movies and stuff, whenever the guy walks the girl home he kisses her." She paused, waiting for me to volunteer some information. When I wasn't forthcoming with any details she asked, "Did you kiss her?"

"Well," I said as I scooted closer to her. "I *did* walk her home. And when we got to her door, she closed her eyes and tilted her head." Ruthie was shaking. I didn't know whether she was cold, angry, or nervous. Maybe she was a little of all three. I saw it as an opportunity. I took my jacket off, put it around her shoulders. I gently lifted her hair out from under the collar and let my hand linger on her back. She must have spent hours fixing her hair -- long ringlets hung down her back. I never understood the logic in straightening her hair just to curl it again, but it looked wonderful.

"Hmph," she said again.

"So I leaned in," I continued as I moved closer to her. My lips were practically touching her ear. "But when I closed my eyes, all I saw was your face. And I wanted you to be my first kiss, not her."

Ruthie turned to me, making our noses touch. She smiled the most beautiful smile I'd ever seen, and then she granted my wish. It was just a little peck, but her lips were so soft. She tasted like vanilla, which I thought was ironic since as a child I had imagined she would taste like chocolate or caramel. There was a tingle in my stomach, and for a second I thought I was going to throw up on her. But then I realized that tingle was love. I was in love with her.

I realize now I was just a kid when that happened, but I felt so grown up. I felt like I could take on anything. Suddenly my home life and my family situation didn't matter. Ruthie *was* my family.

"Do you think we'll always be like this?" she asked as we walked, hand in hand, through the trees to her cottage. She was still wearing my tuxedo jacket, which was huge on her. It was adorable. Every few steps she would step into a ray of moonlight that would reveal once again how beautiful she was. I knew exactly what she meant. She wanted to know if things would always be this perfect, if we would always have each other. I couldn't think of anything poetic or romantic to say. I was still kind of flustered and tingly. So, I stopped walking, pulled her close to me and kissed her again. That was enough of an answer for her.

That night I started to save money. First, I saved any pocket change my father gave me and when I got a job at the local pizza place, I saved nearly every cent of my pay, as well. I called it "My Ruthie Fund". I wanted to buy her a ring. Not any time soon, but when we were old enough, of course. But I knew that I was going to marry her. I didn't care what anyone thought. From that point on we knew that we belonged to each other.

"What are you so happy about?" my mother asked as I entered the kitchen. She dried her hands on a towel, gave me a quick hug, and then went back to washing dishes.

"Nothing, just happy, I guess." I sat down at the table and stared out the back window as if I could see Ruthie's cottage through the trees.

"So I guess your date with Mary Elizabeth went well," she said, smiling. It was kind of odd to see my mother smiling. I don't think I'd seen her smile since Matthew died.

"Actually, I wasn't thinking about Mary Elizabeth."

"Really? Then what are you thinking about?"

This could be my chance. Should I tell her how I felt about Ruthie? Maybe she would tell me that I wasn't crazy for being in love with a colored girl. Maybe she'd tell me everything would work out. But then again, maybe she'd just tell my father and I'd end up with another beating. I decided to test the waters first.

"Mother, what do you think about whites and coloreds marrying?"

A crash echoed in the kitchen as my mother dropped a dish. I rushed to her side to help her clean it up.

"It's illegal," she said, as I picked up the pieces of the broken plate. Her shaky voice was a combination of anger and fear. I didn't understand what brought about these emotions; I thought she liked Ruthie.

"No, it's not. Virginia made it legal three years ago. I checked." I put the shattered plate in the trash can and watched as my mother nervously twisted a dish towel in her hands. She looked absolutely petrified. I approached her and tried to put my arm around her. "Mother, what's wrong?"

She jerked away from me. "Stephen, I think you should stay away from Ruthie, okay? It's better that way.

64

Safer. It's safer that way." She tried to run away, but I pulled her back to me.

"What do you mean, safer? Safe from what?"

She shook her head frantically. "He'll kill us all." She wriggled free from my grasp and charged out of the kitchen. She ran to her room where she cried for the rest of the night.

# Chapter 9

"What's that? What are you pouring into that…that…whatever you call it?" Ruthie asked. She sat on my kitchen counter and watched as I worked on my science project. It was months before anyone would even start thinking about the science fair, but I had to be ready. I had already won three years in a row and I wanted to make sure my streak continued. This year I was working with Chemistry. I wanted to see if I could use regular kitchen ingredients to create a solvent that would strip paint. All she heard when I explained to her my experiment was the word 'paint' and she wanted to join me. "This is a beaker and this is citric acid. Right now I'm trying to increase the acidic level with –"

"Why is that paper changing colors?" Ruthie interrupted me pointing to the counter where I had laid out various strips of litmus paper.

"Because it's litmus paper and…"

"What kind of paints are you using? Water-based or oil-based?" Ruthie started to giggle. She really thought she was getting to me with her questions. She didn't realize that I could never be annoyed with her.

I walked up to her and stood between her legs, silencing her with a kiss. She placed her fingers in my hair and pulled me closer.

"Does that answer your questions?" I asked when I let her up for air.

She smiled and gave me another peck on the lips. I went back to mixing my chemicals.

"So when is your father getting back?"

Why did she always have to bring up my father? I hated thinking about him when I was with her.

"He said he'd be back for dinner." Ruthie looked at her watch. She wanted to make sure she was long gone before then.

"Can I make a suggestion?" Ruthie said after a few minutes. "As someone who uses paints pretty often, there are many low-cost, simple ways to strip paint or clean it off completely. I don't think this project is going to come up with anything incredible."

"Really?" I asked. "So what's your suggestion?"

"Well, from what I can see, you've already come up with about seven really acidic solutions. Why don't you do an experiment to see what substances they can eat through? I think that would be more interesting."

"Why do you think that would be more interesting?"

"Well, let's say you find a combination of regular kitchen ingredients that can eat through metal," she said, hopping off of the kitchen counter. She had that look in her eye that she always got when she came up with a new adventure. I knew the next words to come out of her mouth were going to be imaginative. "Then let's say we get unlawfully locked up in a Turkish prison. We're sentenced to thirty years to life. Our only chance for freedom is to find something that will eat through the metal bars so that we can crawl through and escape and all we have to work with is what they feed us in the mess hall."

"What were we doing in Turkey?" I asked. Ruthie sighed, knowing that once again I had sucked the life out of one of her adventures with my practicality.

"We're on vacation."

"Why are we vacationing in Turkey and what exactly did we do to deserve life in prison?"

"You ask too many questions," she said, laughing.

"*I* ask too many questions?" I asked, thinking back to when she was purposely trying to annoy me. "I just want to make sure that everything makes sense."

"Fine, we get sent to prison for killing..." Ruthie stopped mid-sentence and looked around the kitchen. I could tell she was thinking about Matthew. She blinked away tears and sat down on a stool. We both got quiet. We were fifteen.

Matthew had died ten years ago, yet he was still present in our minds.

"I'm gonna go home, now," she said, hopping off the stool. I stepped in her path and blocked the door.

"Don't go," I said as I grabbed her and held her tight. I kissed the side of her face over and over. "Look, my father won't be home for another two hours. Let me make you something to eat and we can just sit and talk for a while. Okay? Please?"

Ruthie nodded as she wiped the tears from her face After she hopped back up on the counter, I made ham sandwiches and we just talked about my science experiment.

"So what do you think?" Ruthie asked after restating her idea.

"I think it's brilliant. I could use just five different kitchen substances, place a piece of metal in each, and see if the metal loses any mass over time. How long should I let them sit?" I loved this. I loved that we could talk like this. And it didn't hurt that it was about my favorite subject. Ruthie finished her sandwich and started to look around the kitchen for something else to snack on.

"Well, considering that a prisoner would have all the time in the world practically, you should let them sit for a pretty long time. I would say a few months," she said as she opened and closed cabinets.

"But what happens if I devote three months to this experiment and nothing happens?"

"Well, you always say that it's the process that matters. So, you would still have a project." Ruthie gave up on looking for food and started fiddling with the radio.

"But that's not enough to win. I want to win."

"Winning isn't everything, Stephen."

"Let's hear you say that during your next art contest," I said. Ruthie smiled and kept turning the dial on the radio. Then it hit me. "That's it!" I yelled so loudly, Ruthie nearly jumped out of her skin.

"What's it?"

"The radio. Electricity. I can add an electric current to the acid to speed up the process. You're a genius." I picked her up and swung her around. Then we spontaneously started swaying to the Marvin Gaye song that was on. Her arms reached around my neck as Marvin intoned the words of *Mercy Mercy Me*. My hands slipped under her shirt and rubbed her soft, warm skin.

"What's going on here?" my father asked as he walked into the kitchen. He had a peculiar expression on his face. It was like he didn't even really see us; like he was looking through us at a different time. He looked around at all my equipment lying around the kitchen and he started to shake. It was as if he was genuinely afraid. "What are you doing to her?" He spit the words at me viciously. Ruthie wriggled out of my arms and headed for the door. My father grabbed her by the arm. "Did he hurt you?" he asked as he held on to her.

"Stephen would never hurt me, sir. Honest." Ruthie answered sheepishly. She gave me a confused glance, asking for an explanation, but I was just as confused as she was. She was trying to wriggle out of his grasp. Finally, she succeeded and bolted out of the back door. My father stood there for a few minutes, staring at where she had been, and then he walked right past me and headed to his bedroom. He didn't say another word.

I didn't understand his reaction. Why would he think I was trying to hurt Ruthie? The way he looked at her was...was...I don't know what it was. It was almost as if he was looking through her and into another time, and into some secret past. I didn't know if I really wanted to know that secret.

# Chapter 10

I had no idea what went through my father's head. All I knew for sure was that he didn't want me with Ruthie. He could see that his attempt to set me up with Mary Elizabeth had failed miserably. For two years she continued to call and try to find ways for us to meet up together, but I always found an excuse to avoid her. We never became a couple, so my father had to find another way to put an end to the feelings Ruthie and I shared.

"Ruth is going away for the summer," he said on the last day of my sophomore year of high school.

My spoon clattered in my cereal bowl. "What are you talking about?"

My father spun around on me. "Don't question me, boy."

"I'm sorry, Father." I cast my eyes downward, afraid to meet his menacing glare.

He straightened his shoulders then reached for a coffee mug from the cupboard. "Ruth is a very talented artist," he said. "It's about time she developed that talent."

I was afraid to ask what he meant. Thankfully, he continued.

"I'm paying for a program at an art school in New York. She'll be gone for six weeks."

"Six weeks!" I leapt from my chair. How could she be gone for six weeks? We hadn't been apart for more than two days our entire lives. I didn't know if I could live without her for six weeks. What was I going to do?

Sure that my reaction would spark a violent tirade from my father, I braced myself for a blow to the face, but it didn't come.

Instead, he looked down and said, "It's for the best."

One look shared with Ruthie after English class that day was enough of a sign - she knew we needed to talk. We met during lunch, in the woods a block away from school.

"Six weeks?" I said, folding her into my arms as soon as we were alone.

"I know. I know. I have no idea why he's doing this. What is he thinking?"

"I'll tell you what he's thinking. He's trying to keep us apart," I said, squeezing her tightly.

"How can he be trying to keep us apart when he doesn't even know we're together?" She pulled away and looked at me with panic in her eyes before saying, "You haven't told him anything have you?"

"No, of course not. If my father knew what I felt for you, I'd be dead right now." That was the wrong choice of words. Ruthie turned away and hugged herself. "That's not what I meant," I said placing my hands on her shoulders and kissing the top of her head.

"You're right," she said, shaking her head. "We're stepping into dangerous territory, Stephen. Stealing kisses by the lake as children is one thing, but we're getting older now. We're going to be sixteen."

"So?" I didn't know what she was trying to say, but I didn't like her tone. "You're not seriously considering going are you?"

She didn't answer at first. I spun her around so that I was looking in her eyes. "Stephen, we don't have a future together. There's just no way. Maybe some time apart would be good for us. Maybe if we see that there are other things out there –"

"I don't care what else is out there. I only want you." I leaned down to kiss her, but she turned away. My lips landed on her cheek.

"I know that's what you think, but look at us. We're hiding in the woods just so we can talk. You can't even tell your father about us."

"Is that what you want? I'll tell him today if it will make you stay."

She shook her head. "Your father scares me. I don't know what he'd do if he knew. I also don't know what he'd do if I reject his offer."

She took a step away from me. I watched the sunlight trickle through the trees and dance on her face, bringing in shadows of doubt. Or was it something else? Maybe she just didn't love me as much as I loved her. Or maybe my father had gotten to her.

"He said something to you, didn't he? Did he threaten you?" Through all the years of abuse from my father, I had never even considered fighting back in my own defense. But if he'd threatened my Ruthie, I think I would be angry enough to kill him.

"No, he didn't threaten me. But what he did say made a lot of sense." Leaves crunched under her feet as she paced around me. "He probably didn't tell you how prestigious this school is. I had to be accepted before your father could even offer to pay. I can't pass up this opportunity."

I sat down on the ground and ran my fingers through my hair. I couldn't believe she was planning on leaving me for six weeks. What was I supposed to do without her?

"I think I should go," she said after several minutes of pacing.

I shook my head. "No, no. Don't do this. This is just what he wants."

Ruthie knelt in front of and cupped my face in her hands. "It's only six weeks, Stephen. And in that time, please try to find... something else you're passionate about."

I continued to shake my head.

"Just try, okay? And if, in six weeks, we still feel the same way about each other -"

I interrupted her with a kiss so strong it showed her without a doubt where my passion was. I didn't want to stop kissing her. How could she deprive me of her lips for six weeks? I didn't think I could bear it.

Ruthie placed her hands on my chest and pushed me away firmly. Then she ran out of the woods, wiping tears from her eyes.

The next day she was gone.

# Chapter 11

"I think I know what's going on here," Lieutenant Drake said. "Your father was in love with Ruthie. He's been trying to keep you apart all these years because he wants her for himself." He gave a satisfied grin as if he'd unearthed some big mystery. He could dig for days into my father's disturbed psyche and still be nowhere near the truth.

"Did he touch her or something?" he continued. "Is that why you killed him? He touched your girlfriend, you couldn't control your rage, and you killed him in a fit of jealousy."

I sighed and rolled my eyes. "No, that's not it," I said, putting my head in my hands. I should have just let him think that. It would have been easier than what I would eventually have to tell him. But I couldn't let him think that about Ruthie. Not my pure, perfect Ruthie.

There was a rapid knock on the door.

"Lieutenant Drake," a blonde woman said after poking her head into the room. "We finally got in touch with a Stanley Pender from the Livingston police department. Do you want to talk to him? Maybe to corroborate his story?"

My head bolted upright. Lieutenant Drake scooted his chair back and started to stand.

My heartbeat accelerated. My breath caught. I couldn't let him talk to Officer Pender. Not yet, anyway. "How can you corroborate my story when you haven't gotten all of it?" I asked, hoping it would be enough. All I needed was a few more hours.

Lieutenant Drake looked at his watch. I didn't have a watch, but I knew it had to be at least three in the morning.

"Sarah, why don't you tell him to go back to sleep and we'll talk to him in the morning."

"Sure thing," Sarah said before exiting the room.

I exhaled and relaxed a little.

"So where were we?" the lieutenant asked, scooting closer to the table. "Right, you never answered my question. Did your father somehow hurt Ruthie? Is that why you killed him?"

I shook my head. "My father would never hurt Ruthie. He loved her more than he loved me."

"So I'm right. You were jealous of your father's feelings for her and that's why you killed him."

I shook my head again. "I thought you didn't think I killed him. I thought you said I wasn't capable."

"I don't. But given the right circumstances people can be driven to do uncharacteristic things."

I stared down at my hands. Uncharacteristic? What was my character? Sometimes I didn't know who or what I was, let alone what my character was.

"We had an agreement, Stephen," Lieutenant Drake said after a few minutes. "Keep talking."

"When Ruthie left me that summer," I said, "I thought I'd go insane. I didn't think I would survive."

"How did you?"

"Julius," was my only response.

"Who's that?"

# Chapter 12

Ruthie wanted me to find something else I was passionate about? Just how was I supposed to do that? I could barely function without her. Three days after she'd left I still hadn't even gotten out of bed. How was I supposed to find anything?

"I made you some lunch," my mother said, poking her head in after a quick knock. She set the food on my dresser then came over and sat on my bed. I just stared at the ceiling. "I know you miss her, sweetheart." She ran her fingers through my hair. "But you can't let that wanting in your heart be the end of you."

"You don't understand, Mother." I rolled over, turning away from her.

"I understand more than you know," she said with a quiver in her voice.

I turned back around to look at her.

"I was in love once."

I was about to ask her if it was with my father, but somehow I knew that would be a stupid question. I could look at them together and know there had never been any love between them. I leaned up on my elbow and waited for her to continue.

"When he was taken from me... I thought I would die."

Silence enveloped the room as I tried to decipher what she was trying to say. When was this great tragic love of hers? How did she end up in the arms of my father?

"In any case," she said, shaking off her sadness, "Ruthie will be back."

"But, I thought you wanted me to stay away from her?"

My mother got a faraway look in her eyes. "I remember love," she said, before leaving my room.

At least I knew I wasn't alone in this. It gave me a little strength to know that my mother understood what I was going through. And she was right. I could get through this. Ruthie would be back in just six weeks.

I swung my feet over the edge of the bed and scarfed down the lunch Mother had made. Then I decided to go for a walk.

I ended up on the other side of town in what was known as the black area. I don't know how I got there. I must have been daydreaming as I walked. Most white boys my age would have been afraid to be caught in this part of town.

I could feel the stares as I walked down McDowell Street and past the housing projects. Truth be told, I was little lost, but I just kept walking anyway until I could find something I recognized. I finally came across the city park. It wasn't the same park that Matthew used to take Ruthie and me to, but we had driven past it a couple of times. I wasn't lost anymore, but I decided to take a break before I started home.

There was a group of guys playing basketball, so I ended up watching them for a while. I had never played basketball before; I don't know why. I guess it was because I really didn't have any guy friends and a game of hoops had never quite made it on Ruthie's adventure list. I stood at the fence and watched those guys play for nearly an hour. It looked like fun. It couldn't be too hard to do.

The next morning I went and bought a basketball. I couldn't believe I didn't already own one. I was probably the only teenage boy who had never owned a basketball. I got to the court before anyone else and started shooting around, until I heard someone laughing. I turned to see a tall, skinny, black kid in shorts and a T-shirt.

"You shoot like my brother," he said. From his tone of voice I could tell it wasn't a compliment. "My brother's a nerd. He shoots like a girl." He stepped onto the court and shot from about three feet behind where I was standing. It went in with a swoosh. Nothing but net.

"I'm Julius," he said when he approached me. "And if you keep shooting like that you're gonna get killed out here." I had no idea that I was doing anything wrong.

"Can you show me?"

"I guess I have to. I don't wanna to be responsible for any dead white boys." He took the ball away from me. "First of all, you don't shoot with two hands. One hand is always higher than the other. One hand supports the ball while the other hand guides it into the goal." He demonstrated it, then handed the ball over for me to try. I got my hands into the right position and took a shot. It hit the backboard with a thud and returned almost right to me.

"I guess I didn't do it right."

"No, your form was good. Let me tell you a little secret. It doesn't matter as much if your shot goes in or not, as long as you look fly while ya shootin' it. Let's work on gettin' the look down, now, so you don't look like a silly white boy while you're out here. We'll work on gettin' it to go in another day." Julius spent the next couple of hours showing me how to look "fly" while I played basketball. Not many of my shots actually went in. A little after one o'clock, other people started to arrive. They already had an even number, so I didn't get to play, but I still stayed and watched. Julius was right. Everyone out there looked "fly". They each had a certain finesse with the ball and a confidence that seemed to will every shot to go in, whether it did or not.

There was a lot I had to learn if I wanted to play with these guys. I needed to practice. Thankfully, Julius was willing to help. We spent nearly three hours every morning working on my shots. I bought a basketball goal and put it up at my house so I could practice at home after dark. I became obsessed with the game. It was the only thing that took my mind off of Ruthie.

A few days later, some guys were one short so they let me play. They must have thought it was some sort of initiation, the way slammed into me every chance they got. They were surprised when I kept getting back up. I even blocked two shots and made six points. It was a pretty impressive showing for my first time. As I was leaving, one of the older boys shouted, "See ya tomorrow, kid!" It was the biggest compliment they could have paid me. I was being included.

I was so busy playing it cool and pretending that the invitation hadn't made my day that I didn't notice Julius running up behind me.

"Hey, you wanna come to my house for dinner? My mom's a great cook."

Julius lived in a two-bedroom apartment with his younger brother and sister. I had no idea how they managed to fit five people in such a cramped space. My house had six bedrooms, a formal dining room, living room, den, sun room, and porch and I still felt trapped sometimes. But that could have been for different reasons.

"This is my little brother, Timothy. The one who shoots like a girl." Timothy gave his brother a hurt look, but Julius just laughed. Timothy looked very familiar, but I couldn't quite figure out where I'd seen him.

"You're Ruthie's friend aren't you?"

I nodded, although I really wanted to say that we were more than friends. Suddenly, I felt very possessive of Ruthie.

"Where is she? I haven't seen her around lately," Timothy asked. He was a little too interested in my Ruthie, but he looked harmless. Julius was right. He was a nerd.

"Yeah, he's had no one to fantasize about since she's been gone," Julius said with his trademark grin. Timothy didn't find it funny. Neither did I. Then it hit me.

"You're in my physics class!" I said suddenly and then promptly went into a sneezing fit. They must have had pets. I was allergic to pets. Most pets, that is.

"Oh, no, not you, too?" Julius said, tossing me a roll of toilet paper so I could wipe my nose. "Are you as big a nerd as he is?" He shrugged. "Oh well, at least you can ball."

Dinner at Julius's house was fun. It was the first time I could remember laughing at the dinner table. I loved the way Julius interacted with his younger brother and sister. He teased them a lot, but it was always good-natured. They could tell that underneath his sarcastic façade he really loved them. It kind of made me wish I had a brother or sister.

I sat by the phone every night, willing it to ring, hoping that Ruthie would call, but she never did. I thought about her constantly, wondering if she had found someone else to love.

If my father thought sending her away for the summer would make me forget about her, he was sadly mistaken. I felt like a part of me had been savagely ripped away from my body. At first basketball helped to ease the pain, but I quickly learned that it only masked it. Especially when I constantly heard boys on the basketball court talk about how beautiful Ruthie was and how nearly every guy in town had asked her out over the past couple of years, but she always said no.

My aching for Ruthie grew every moment. By the time the day came for her to return I thought I would explode. I sat on my front porch, trying to look casual as I waited for the taxicab that would bring her back to me. I flipped through a book, the title of which I can't even remember, and looked down the road every ten seconds.

At 3:17 in the afternoon, it finally came. In my dreams, I imagined that the taxi would pull up in front of my house; Ruthie would leap out, jump into my arms, and kiss me with six weeks' worth of bottled-up passion. But that didn't happen. I watched Ruthie stare straight ahead as the taxi drove right past my house and toward her cottage.

I stormed into the house and threw my book across the room. I guess it happened. I guess Ruthie had found someone else and didn't care about me anymore. How could she not want to see me as soon as she returned? If she missed me half as much as I missed her, she would have jumped out of that car before it even stopped moving.

"Reverend?" my mother asked, stepping out of the kitchen. She must have heard the book crash and thought my father had come home angry.

"No, it's just me, Mother."

My mother clutched her chest in relief. "Oh, okay. I'm going to go lay down for a few moments before he gets here."

She headed upstairs as I plopped on the sofa, prepared to wallow in my own misery. A few minutes later, I heard a knock on the back door. It was Ruthie. It had to be. I jumped up and ran to answer it. Sure enough, it was her.

"Hi, Stephen," she said when I swung open the screen door.

"Hi," I said, still hoping she would leap into my arms at any second.

We stared at each other in silence, as if we were strangers.

Finally, Ruthie said, "I bought a gift for your parents...from New York." She held up a package, but didn't try to enter the house.

"Oh, uh, my mother is asleep and my father isn't home."

"He isn't?" she asked with eyebrows raised.

"No, he –"

Before I could finish my thought, Ruthie wrapped her arms around my neck and kissed me hungrily. I picked her up and clutched her thighs in my hands as we stumbled into the kitchen.

"I've missed you so much," she said, taking a second to pull away. She wrapped her legs around me and pressed her body into mine. "I'm so sorry I didn't call you. He told me not to." She pressed her lips to mine again.

I knew she was referring to my father. I don't know what he said to her to convince her to stay away from me, but it obviously didn't have any permanent effects.

"Never leave me again," I pleaded as I laid her on the kitchen table.

"I won't. I can't," she said with tears in her eyes. "I can't live without you anymore, Stephen."

I crawled on top of her while slipping my hands under her shirt. I kissed her neck, her cheeks, her eyes, her lips. When my hands undid her bra and massaged her breasts, she moaned my name. I didn't know if I would be able to stop. I thought I was going to take her right there on the kitchen table. That was until we both heard a car door slam.

"Your father!" she said, bolting up right nearly knocking me over. She jumped off the table and headed for the door.

I grabbed her arm and pulled her back to me. I wanted to ask her to stay, but not with my father coming. There's no telling what he would do if he caught us like this. I didn't care about myself, but I couldn't put Ruthie in danger.

I kissed her again - slowly, passionately - and then said, "I'm coming over tonight. Leave your window open."

I don't know what I expected her to say. Well, I expected her to say no. Ruthie was completely against sex before marriage. I remembered the countless moments of frustration I felt when she'd push me away if we started going too far. So I certainly didn't expect her to say, "Okay," before dashing out the door.

# Chapter 13

Dinner with my parents lasted a lifetime that night. The normal silence and clattering of cutlery was almost unbearable. I tried to make the time pass more quickly by thinking about the fact that in just a few short hours I would be sharing a bed with my Ruthie, but the anticipation made it worse.

Father never made any attempt at conversation during dinner. Sometimes I wondered if he even liked us. It would have been such a blessing if my father one day decided to just up and leave. He wouldn't be missed.

The torment of a family meal finally ended when my father scooted his chair away from the table. That was the cue that we were released from our obligation of spending time together.

I think I cleared my dishes and was halfway to my room before my father even stood up all the way.

"Are you alright, Stephen?" my mother called after me.

"I'm fine. Just going to bed early. I have an early start at work tomorrow." At least one of them should have picked up on this obvious lie. I had worked at a Leonard's Pizza Palace all summer. Not exactly the type of establishment that opened early and served breakfast. Apparently neither of my parents cared enough about me to even question it.

An hour later, I heard my parents go into their room. It was after midnight when I felt they were in a deep enough sleep for me to sneak out of the house unnoticed.

I didn't have to crawl through Ruthie's bedroom window that night. She left the front door open for me. I followed the glow of candlelight and the sound of *These Arms of Mine* by Otis Redding. When I got to her room, Ruthie lay on top of the sheets in a yellow nightgown, sleeping peacefully. She must have drifted off while she was waiting for me.

I took off my shirt and my shoes, crawled in the bed and wrapped my arms around her waist. When I kissed her neck, her eyes fluttered open.

She turned toward me and said, "I thought you weren't coming. I thought maybe your father –"

"Shh," I said placing my fingers over her lips. "Let's not think about him. Not tonight."

My hand slid under her nightgown. I felt her melt under my caress. She raised her arms so I could undress her. My heartbeat accelerated at the sight of her naked body.

"I'm so scared, Stephen," she said while kissing my bare chest.

"Do you want to stop?" I asked, praying she wouldn't say yes.

"No. I'm afraid this isn't real. It feels so good to be with you. It feels too good to be true. Just kiss me and prove to me I'm not dreaming."

I kissed her so powerfully then that she couldn't help but know that this was real, that *we* were real.

When we finished making love, Ruthie started crying. I held her tightly against me as her tears rained on my chest.

"What's wrong?" I whispered, after kissing the top of her head. "Did I hurt you? Do you regret being with me?"

She shook her head. "No, it's not that. It's just... I love you so much, Stephen."

"I love you, too." I lifted her head so I could look into her eyes and said, "Marry me."

"Okay."

*** 

The next two weeks were the best of my life. Most nights we would make love and then fall asleep in each other's arms. Sometimes though, we just held each other while making plans for the future.

We made sure to stay away from each other during the day. We both thought that if my father got one glimpse of us, he'd know what we were doing just by the looks on our faces. Instead, we met at the local library where Ruthie worked in the afternoon.

We had our time together there down to a science. At 4:15, the librarian would go to the bathroom. I don't know what she did in there, but it gave us a good twenty minutes of alone time. Ruthie would only have to give me a look and I knew the time was getting close. She'd grab a few books and walk toward the reference section as if she was going to restack them. I would walk in the other direction and meet her there.

"School starts tomorrow," she said while I kissed her neck. I had set her on top of a low bookcase and stood between her legs.

"Uh huh," I grunted, not removing my lips from her body. I didn't feel like talking.

"So are things going to change?"

I pulled away from her and looked in her eyes. "No, of course not. How could you think that?"

She looked down. "It's not going to be easy for you, Stephen. Do you know what names you're going to be called if people find out you're in love with me?"

"I don't care. They can call me whatever they want. It's not going to change what I feel for you."

Ruthie shook her head. "What if someone at school tells your father?"

She had a good point. I didn't care if people at school knew about us, but my father was a different story. There's no telling what he would do.

Ruthie misinterpreted my silence. "You're not ready for this, Stephen. If you want to keep our relationship a secret for a little while longer, I understand."

I didn't know what to say, so I just hugged her. I didn't want her to think I was ashamed of her, but I also didn't want my father to find out. I felt trapped.

It was probably best if we kept our love a secret, but what happened the next day at school changed everything.

# Chapter 14

I planned on playing it cool in school the next day. Nothing really had changed. I had always loved Ruthie and I knew she loved me. The only difference was that we shared a bed. Technically that was a big change, but just for us. No one else needed to know.

School should have proceeded as normal. Ruthie and I always got by with the same secret smiles and nods of acknowledgement during the day. If we needed to speak, we'd sneak off to the woods during lunch. We never spoke at school. Never. We didn't want to arouse suspicion.

It wasn't that whites and Negros didn't talk or anything at school. It was just that interracial dating was a bit taboo. No one did it - not publicly, anyway. If there were interracial couples, I didn't know about it.

After first period I headed toward Ruthie's locker just so I could get a glimpse of her. I thought maybe I could accidently bump into her, as well, just so I could touch her.

When I turned the corner, I saw Bruce Connelly leaning on the locker next to Ruthie's. He was smiling and rubbing the patch of blond hair poking out of his plaid shirt that was unbuttoned nearly to his navel. I didn't like Bruce, and not just because he was currently leering at my girlfriend, but because I'd heard him in the locker room on several occasions saying that colored girls were only good for one thing.

My hands balled into fists. I didn't know what I was going to do, but I knew I couldn't tolerate him looking at Ruthie like that for much longer. I tried to take a deep breath and calm down. They were just talking. It was no big deal. But then he reached out and tucked a stray hair behind her ear. He was doing more than talking. I recognized that look in his eyes. He wanted my Ruthie.

What in the world was going on? I thought whites and Negros together was too taboo for our school. Maybe it wasn't. Maybe that was just in my imagination. Had I just been too scared all this time? If Bruce was brave enough to hit on Ruthie in public, why wasn't I brave enough to... do something? I didn't know what, but I knew I had to somehow show what I felt for Ruthie.

Before I knew what was happening, my feet carried me over to them. I stood there with my fists tightened and my jaw clenched, too conflicted to know what to actually say. I couldn't really kick Bruce's ass for touching my girl. No one knew she was my girl. I think it was time I changed that.

"Hey, man," Bruce said after a few minutes of me just standing there awkwardly. "What's up?" He held his hand out for me to give him "five" but I just stared at it.

"Um, Stephen," Ruthie said, trying to snap me out of my trance. "Bruce was just inviting me to a party this weekend." She tried to sound cheery but I think she knew how angry I was.

"You can come, too, man. I just didn't think you were the partying type, ya' know. I mean, there won't be any microscopes or anything there." Bruce chuckled. I didn't crack a smile as I stared at him. He straightened his posture and poked out his chest, suddenly aware that he might be in danger.

"Come on, Ruthie. I'll walk you to class." I grabbed her hand and entwined our fingers together, not breaking my eye contact with Bruce.

Ruthie didn't move at first. I looked at her and saw how she stared down at our hands with her mouth open. Then she raised her head and looked into my eyes in complete shock. Slowly, her lips curved into a smile. I knew she was happy.

I pulled her away from her locker and a stunned Bruce Connelly toward her next class.

Ruthie squeezed my hand as we walked, ignoring the stares and whispers. "Today 'little black boys and little black girls will be able to join hands with little white boys and little white girls as sisters and brothers,'" she said when we reached her art class. She thought the day we dreamed about when we were five years old and listening to Dr. Martin Luther King had finally come. Feeling the tension in the pit of my stomach, I wasn't so sure.

Maybe it was too soon for me to profess my feelings for Ruthie like this. It might seem like a simple thing, but holding hands like that in the hallway was the equivalent of asking for a marriage license.

Ruthie sensed my apprehension. She grabbed my other hand and said, "I love you, Stephen. We're going to be okay."

"I love you, too," I said, staring down at her. But something inside me screamed that we *weren't* going to be okay.

# Chapter 15

That night while I was sleeping, my father came into my room and beat me with a broomstick. I was so disorientated that I couldn't defend myself. I tried to get up, but I was too weak after the first few blows. He kept yelling things like "stay away from her" and "never disobey me". Right before I passed out I thought I heard him call her a nigger.

By the time I woke up the next day it was too late for me to go to school. At first, I didn't remember what happened. Then I tried to move. Every inch of me was in pain. It hurt to even breathe.

Thankfully, nothing was broken. I didn't want to have to go to the hospital again. My mother and I had been there so many times I had lost count. I was tired of the looks. It was too far away, as well - we never went to the one in town. We always drove two hours away and went to an emergency room in a town that was even smaller than ours. We gave fake names and paid with cash. It was only in the direst situations that we made the effort to go, like right after my father murdered Matthew and my mother was vomiting blood. I didn't understand what the word miscarriage meant back then. When I found out, I was more than a little terrified. That meant that my father had killed two of my siblings and it was only a matter of time before he got to me. I thought that time had come last night, but I had survived once again.

I lay in bed and tried to make sense of it all. But I couldn't. There was no logic to it. All we had done was hold hands in the hallway at school. It was something any two teenagers in love should have been allowed to do, but because of our skin color it was unacceptable.

Around three o'clock I stumbled out of bed. I was weak and light-headed, but I had to get out of that house. I had to see Ruthie. My mother made me eat something so that I wouldn't pass out while I was driving.

"He's afraid. He never had the life he wanted and he takes it out on us," she said. She put some food on my plate and handed it to me as I gingerly sat down at the table.

"What is he afraid of?" She didn't answer me. Instead, she came up behind me and put her arms around my shoulders. She kissed my head and just said she was sorry over and over again.

"You really love her, don't you?" she asked moments later.

"I do, Mother. It's like she's the reason I wake up in the morning. Without her, I'd die." She touched my chin and turned my face toward hers.

"Then love her no matter what he tells you."

I got washed up, shaved, and tried to make myself look presentable so that Ruthie wouldn't worry. I got to the library right around 4:15.

"Where were you today? I was worried." Ruthie had been standing by the door of the library, hoping I would show up. We walked hand in hand to our favorite hidden spot between the stacks.

"You missed my unveiling. Are you okay?" The unveiling was a big event for all the art students. Usually in the spring there would be an exhibit featuring all their work from the year. The art teacher really just started it as a way to showcase Ruthie, and this year she added a fall exhibit to display the work Ruthie had done in New York over the summer.

With all of our plans to get married I had completely forgotten about it, but at least she had shown me her paintings beforehand. The best of her work this year was a painting she called "Into the Light." She had painted a person walking into a ray of light, using only shades of yellow. Thirty-seven shades of yellow to be exact. I didn't even know thirty-seven shades of yellow existed. It was a very powerful painting. When I first looked at it, I thought it represented happiness because of all the yellow. After staring at it for a while, I saw that it was really a dark and foreboding painting that made me think about death.

"Yeah, I'm fine - I'm sorry I missed it. I had to...take my mom to the hospital today, that's all." I lied. "I'll make it up to you, I promise." That was the truth. I *would* find a way to make it up to her.

"Don't worry about it. Is your mother okay?"

"Yeah, she's fine. It was nothing."

"What did he do to her this time?" Ruthie grimaced as if she could feel the pain herself. She was always so empathetic. I loved that about her.

"He...um." There were a million things that I could have said he did. All of which would have been true at some point. I just always had a hard time lying to Ruthie.

"I don't want to talk about it," I said, finally. "This is our time."

"Okay. Has your father find out about us, yet? I'm sure someone probably told him about the hand-holding by now," she said as she came close to me and kissed me gently on the lips. When she hugged me I must have winced in pain.

"What? What is it?"

"It's nothing. I'm fine." She didn't believe me. She started to unbutton my shirt. I grabbed her hands to make her stop, but she gave me a fierce look.

"Stephen, let me look at it." When she got my shirt open, she gasped. My chest was nearly completely covered with bruises. I was black and blue all over. She took my shirt completely off and stared at the damage to my back.

"Oh, Stephen," she cried as she gently traced the fresh bruises with her fingertips. "We have to get you to a doctor."

This was the worst beating she had ever seen my father give me. I never let her see when things got too bad. I would always hide in my room for a few days until the wounds healed before I went to see her again.

"I'm fine. Nothing's broken. I would know if something was broken."

"Stephen, you can't go on like this. He's going to kill you. Please get out of that house, if not for your own sake, then for mine. What would I do without you? You're all I have." Tears were streaming down her face, but she was holding back from breaking down completely. I held her in my arms and let the tears fall on my bare chest. I loved to hold her. Taking care of her made me forget my own problems.

"Look, Ruthie, I'm fine. Don't worry about me. It was my fault anyway. I shouldn't have held your hand in public like that. Maybe it was too soon."

"He did this to you because we held hands?" she choked through the tears as she pulled away from me. She was going to blame herself. I couldn't let her do that.

107

"No, Ruthie, it's not your fault."

"I know it's not my fault, Stephen!" she yelled at me. She wiped the tears from her face, trying to get control of her emotions. I tried to quiet her down. Even though the library was completely empty, it still felt weird talking so loudly.

"Ruthie, calm down."

"I will not calm down!" She pushed my hands away when I tried to hug her again.

"Ruthie, please..."

"Stephen, I know it's not my fault and it's not your fault either. But you don't see that. He's got you so brainwashed that you actually think you deserve his torture. I've spent my whole life trying to convince you that you're worth more than that, that you deserve better, but you just don't get it!"

"Shh!" I covered her mouth as an old man came into the library. He glanced around as if he had a question. After a couple of minutes, when no one came to his assistance, he walked back out. I let go of her mouth when she had calmed down a little. She sat on the floor and put her face in her hands.

"I can't do this anymore," she said finally.

"Okay, let's go somewhere else and talk." I thought she meant she couldn't meet me in the library anymore, but it was much more serious than that.

"No, that's not what I mean." She swallowed. "I mean I can't do *us* anymore. I can't sit back and watch him kill you, just like Matthew. I can't take it. I can't watch you die. I can't lose someone else that I love."

"You're not going to lose me. I'll always be here for you. I promise." I held her to me tightly.

Ruthie shook her head. "You can't promise that. Not when you live with that man."

We sat on the ground holding each other for a moment. I had to think of a way to assure her.

"You're right. You're absolutely right. I need to get away from him. But I need you to come with me. Tonight."

Ruthie pulled away and stared at me.

"Tonight?" she said.

"Yes, tonight. Why do we need to wait?" I said, staring into her eyes with a newfound sense of enthusiasm and hope. "I have some money saved up. We can get an apartment. I can get a better job; you can sell some paintings. Let's do it. Let's do it tonight."

Ruthie looked down for a second. I thought she was going to reject me by claiming it was too dangerous, but instead she said, "Let's do it."

We kissed each other with renewed vigor. Even after the librarian came back, we continued to hold and caress each other as we made our plans. We made arrangements to meet after midnight and drive to Washington DC so we could get married as close to where Martin Luther King had made his "I have a Dream" speech as possible. Tonight *our* dream was coming true.

"If you change your mind, I'll understand," Ruthie said as she walked me to my truck. "If you don't come tonight, I'll have my answer and I won't hold it against you."

"Nothing could stop me from being with you."

When I got home my father was waiting for me. He sat in the recliner next to the television and stared into nothingness. I probably could have slipped right past him and gone to my room without him even noticing. But for some reason I felt the need to stand up to him. I was entering a new stage in my life with Ruthie. If I wasn't strong enough to tell my father of my intentions, how would I ever be able to face all the obstacles that Ruthie and I would face?

"Ruthie and I are getting married," I said, bracing myself for the imminent abuse. I started to look around for something I could use for self-defense. I spotted a lamp, a vase, and the same broomstick that he had used on me. That would be poetic justice. That's what I would reach for first. I planned how I would pin him down and demand that he leave me and Ruthie alone.

But he didn't attack me. He didn't even move from his chair. He just folded his hands together and stared into the distance.

"You can't marry her. It's illegal," he said calmly - too calmly.

"No, it's not. Anti-miscegenation laws were repealed in Virginia in 1968."

He shook his head.

"Even if it was still illegal, I would do it anyway. I love her and I'm not letting you or anyone else keep me from her anymore. I don't care that she's Negro -"

"It's not because she's Negro!" he yelled, interrupting me. He stood up and tried to use his size to intimidate me, but I was taller than him. I was proud for a moment that I wasn't afraid of him. I straightened my back and met his evil glare. He bit his bottom lip in frustration. He realized his normal scare tactics weren't going to work this time. He opened his mouth to say something and nothing came out. I wondered what he could possibly say to try to convince me to no longer love Ruthie.

He opened his mouth again and blurted, "It's not because she's Negro. It's because...I'm her father. You two are half brother and sister."

# Chapter 16

Saying it out loud brought back all the emotion from that night. I felt sick to my stomach. I thought I might throw up right there in the interrogation room. I noticed a look of disgust on Lieutenant Drake's face. He took a deep breath and tried to remain professional.

"So, Theodore was Ruthie's father. That's why he'd always had a special interest in her."

I nodded and then I gagged a little.

"Ray, can we get the kid some water?" Lieutenant Drake called through the door.

Seconds later an officer handed me a glass of lukewarm water. I thought about Ruthie as I drank. I wondered if she was in the next room giving her version of events. Of course she didn't know anything about that night. I had spared her the details.

"Thanks," I said, placing the empty glass on the table. I hadn't realized how thirsty I was.

We sat in silence for a moment as I tried to block out images of my past.

Lieutenant Drake closed his eyes and rubbed his temples. I had been talking for three hours and he still wasn't any closer to figuring out who killed my father.

"So is that why you killed him? Not for the years of abuse, but because he told you Ruthie was your..." He trailed off, not even able to finish the sick thought.

"I should have killed him that night. Right then and there. I should've taken that broomstick and jabbed it through his throat. That would've made me feel better."

"But you didn't." He crossed his arms and studied me. "You must have been pretty angry."

I glared at the lieutenant. "I was beyond angry. For sixteen years, that man sat back and watched me fall in love with her. He didn't say a word. He just let it happen. And then with one phrase - she's your sister - he took away everything that meant anything to me."

He nodded in agreement, trying to understand how I felt. "So why didn't you kill him then?"

I shrugged. "I wanted to. I tried. My mother stopped me."

Lieutenant Drake took in a deep breath and let it out slowly. "Tell me about what happened."

# Chapter 17

"That's not true." I said the words but I didn't believe them, even though they left my own mouth. Everything started to make sense. My father only had a problem with Ruthie when he saw me close to her. And all these years he had taken such good care of her. He wasn't obsessed with her. He loved her. He loved her more than he loved me.

"I had an affair with her mother," he said.

My stomach clenched. It was true. I didn't want to believe it, but in my heart I knew it. I hunched over and vomited on the living room floor. My father stood over me silently. I couldn't see his face but I had the feeling that he enjoyed my pain.

When the convulsions stopped, I clutched my stomach and felt the room spin. I couldn't breathe. My legs turned to liquid as I fell to my knees, soiling my pants with my own bile.

"It wasn't my fault," my father said. "She made me fall in love with her."

"What...what are you...talking about?" I asked, momentarily forgetting everything and everyone around me.

My father rubbed his hands together as if he was worried. Something about the truth disturbed him. As if he was afraid for anyone to find out. "Mabel. Ruthie's mother." He started pacing the living room. "She was a nigger. She was supposed to be dumb, lazy, and nasty. But she wasn't any of those things. She was beautiful, smart, and talented. Did you know she was a singer? She had a beautiful voice."

I didn't want to hear any of this. Every word he said to me felt like a dagger, slowly stabbing the life out of me.

"Mabel was your mother's governess," he continued, sitting down on the couch. He suddenly had a nostalgic look in his eyes as he remembered Ruthie's mother. "She moved to town with Marjorie's family. Your mother was a shy, boring, pathetic excuse for a woman. Mabel was the only person she'd talk to. I asked Marjorie out, knowing she would insist Mabel come as a chaperone. Mabel was an enchantress. It wasn't my fault that I fell in love with her."

He stood and paced the living room. "I was the choir director of my father's church at that time. Somehow I convinced him to let Mabel sing with the whites. Every week she stole hearts with her voice. People started coming from miles away just to hear her."

Why was he telling me this? I didn't want to know. I wanted to leave, but I felt like my knees were glued to the carpet. I couldn't move.

"Soon, my father figured out my feelings for Mabel. He tried to beat it out of me. Then he tried to send her away. I couldn't let that happen. So I married your mother in a rushed ceremony a week later. I don't know why your mother agreed to it. I like to think Mabel convinced her. They both moved in after the ceremony. That was Mabel's way of staying close to me. I know it. I know she loved me, too."

I put my face in my hands and shook my head. I didn't want to know. I should have just run away with Ruthie without telling him of our plans. If I didn't know about this dark secret, everything would be okay. It wouldn't matter. But now that I knew, nothing would ever be the same. Unless this was what he wanted. Maybe he was making it up. It was a trick to keep me away from Ruthie.

"You're lying. You're lying," I said over and over again. "You're not her father. You just don't want us to be together."

He shook his head. "It's the truth. She's my daughter. You're my son. I've told you all your life to stay away from her. You should have listened to me." My father stood up. He stood straight and held his head high as if he was completely free from guilt. In his mind he had done nothing wrong. He strutted toward the kitchen as if the conversation was over.

The revulsion building in my stomach abated momentarily, only to be replaced with wrath. "You're blaming me?" I glared at him. He must have felt the fire in

117

my gaze because he stopped and turned around. He was surprised by my vicious tone. "You watched me fall in love with her. For sixteen years you sat back and let it happen." I found some inner reserve of strength and got to my feet. "All you had to do was tell us. Just once. How could you do this?" I stood in front of him, towering over his middle-aged, slightly overweight form. A bead of sweat formed over his eyebrow.

"You best remember who you are, boy." He raised his hand and landed an open-handed slap across my face. Normally, that simple act of brutality would be enough to shut me up. In the past I would have apologized for my tone and headed for my room. Or I would have removed my shirt and waited for him to bring out the whip. But not this time. Something in me had changed. I didn't feel the sting of the slap. I didn't feel sorry for what I'd said.

I felt nothing.

I stared into his eyes. I saw the fear and evil behind them.

"You raped her, didn't you? She didn't love you. No one could love you. You raped her."

His eyes expanded. "I did no such thing." He raised his hand to me again. This time it was a fist coming toward me, but I caught it in midair. His face twisted in pain as I squeezed his fingers together. I pushed his fist into his face. He stumbled backwards and fell against the wall.

I picked up a lamp and raised it above my head. I was going to bash his brains in, right there on the spot.

"Stephen," my mother said softly. Suddenly she was standing right beside me.

I froze.

"Don't do it, baby."

"Why not? He deserves it."

She shook her head. "You don't want to live with that burden."

"I don't want to live at all." I dropped the lamp and went to my room.

# Chapter 18

I lost count of the days I missed from school. Nothing mattered anymore. Ruthie made no attempts to call or come over. I remembered her saying that if I didn't show up that night she'd have her answer about my feelings for her. She probably thought I was too scared to stand up to my father and marry her. If that's what she thought, it was better than the truth.

I came to certain realizations about my life as I lay in bed, staring at the ceiling. First and foremost was that I had no life. I had no goals, no desires, and no future without Ruthie. She was my everything. All my life I imagined we would somehow be together. She was all I had ever wanted. Without her, I was nothing. I had no idea how I would pass the days. What would I think about? What would I do? Who would I talk to? Besides Ruthie, I didn't even have any friends. I had no hobbies, no likes or dislikes, no personality. All my life I had defined myself through Ruthie. Now that I couldn't have her, I had no idea who I was.

"You have to eat," my mother said, suddenly appearing in my room. But then again, she could have been there for hours and I might not have noticed. "You haven't eaten in three days."

I rolled over and stared at her. I really looked at her and studied her as I never had before. She was my mother. She was supposed to love me. She seemed to be a caring person. How could she let this happen?

"Did you know, Mother? Did you know he was her father?"

She looked away. "Yes," she said simply, her head hanging low.

I was too weak to get angry. I just rolled over and turned my back to her.

She reached out and stroked the back of my head. "Look, baby, it doesn't matter. Just run away with her like you planned. No one will ever suspect you're brother and sister."

How could she even suggest such a thing? The thought sickened me. How would I be able to look at myself every day, knowing that I willingly slept with my sister? I couldn't live like that.

Determined never to tell Ruthie, I preferred to let her hate me than to know the truth. I didn't want her to live with the guilt.

Eventually, I went back to school. I don't even remember how I got there. I walked around in a fog. People had to call my name three or four times before I acknowledged them.

Seeing her in the hallway abruptly awakened me from my mindless stupor. She was completely different. There was an air about her like she had matured overnight. And she was hanging off the arm of Anthony Everson, the star running back of the football team. He was groping and touching her right in front of everyone. When I saw him kiss her, I lost it. I ran toward him and tackled him to the floor. How dare he kiss her? We rolled around the hall for a while and then somehow tumbled out the front door and down the steps.

I felt something in my body crack, but I didn't let that stop me. All my built-up anger and aggression exploded onto unsuspecting Anthony, just because he happened to touch my girlfriend - I mean, my sister. Ruthie tried to stop us and pull me off of him, but she was too little to have any effect.

"Break it up. Break it up!" Julius said, pulling me away. He had to use all his strength to keep me from going after Anthony again. "Stephen, man, you need to chill out before the principal or, worse, the police come."

I tried to scramble away from him and get another punch in, but Julius wouldn't let go.

"Stay away from her! She's mine!" I yelled like a raging lunatic.

Julius dragged me away from the front steps of the school.

"Man, I don't know what the hell is wrong with you, but you need to get out of here and calm down," Julius said once we got about a block away from school and he finally let me go.

Ruthie was right behind him.

"God, Stephen, you're bleeding," she said, stepping forward and reaching for my face. I turned away from her.

"That's the cops," Julius said looking down the street at a police car turning into the school parking lot. "Run!"

Julius took off in one direction and I headed to the woods. I probably didn't need to run. Since I was white I could have made up any story I wanted and the police would have believed me. Anthony would have been arrested immediately. I ran because I didn't feel like explaining. I just didn't want to talk about it.

I realized Ruthie was still with me after I was well into the woods. I stopped running, yanked her to me, and crammed my tongue down her throat.

"What the hell is the matter with you?" she yelled as she tried to pull away from my grasp. I held onto her tightly, refusing to let go. I was too strong for her. I stared into her eyes. They were his eyes! They had the exact same light brown eyes. How could I fall in love with someone with *his* eyes? How could I even look at her anymore and not see

124

him? Part of me hated her, now. Part of me wanted to hurt her the way he had hurt me. But the rest of me realized that she was the same beautiful little girl that I had loved all my life.

"You're hurting me!" She started to cry. She slapped me hard across the face. That broke the spell I was under. I let her go and she collapsed onto the ground.

"Stephen, tell me what's wrong. I don't know what to do."

"I'm sorry. I'm so sorry, Ruthie. I didn't mean to hurt you." I fell to the ground and sobbed. This shocked her even more. She had known me all my life, through broken arms, sprained ankles and dislocated shoulders, mostly due to the countless beatings from that man. Never once had she seen me cry. She stared at me in disbelief, not knowing what to do. Then she tentatively came over and wrapped her arms around me. I clung to her like she was going to disappear as she planted kisses on my neck.

"Please talk to me, Stephen. Please, tell me what's going on."

"I love you so much. I don't know what I'm going to do."

"I love you, too."

"We can never be together."

"Why not? If this is about Anthony, I'm sorry. Nothing happened. I was just trying to get back at you for hurting me. For not wanting to marry me. He means nothing. I love *you*."

How was I going to tell her? I didn't know if I could say it out loud. I finally just blurted it out.

"You're my sister!"

"What are you talking about? That's impossible." She let go of me and scooted away.

"My father is your father. He had an affair with your mother. We're half brother and sister."

She stared at me with her mouth agape, as if trying to process the information. She finally stood and turned away. I followed suit and tried to put my hand on her shoulder. She brushed it away.

"I'm sorry, Ruthie. I didn't want to tell you. I thought I could move on without you knowing, but seeing you -"

Suddenly, she turned around and slapped me again. "How dare you?" she said. "I am *not* that man's child." She started to storm away.

I grabbed her arm and pulled her back to me. "It's the truth."

"You're pathetic, Stephen. Just admit you're too scared. Admit you don't love me enough. I hate you!" She struggled loose and ran away.

How could she think I didn't love her? That hurt worse than the slap. Maybe it was better if she hated me.

Maybe that would make it easier for me to move on and forget her.

# Chapter 19

The sound of sirens always struck fear in my soul. I was always afraid the sirens would be for my mother or me. With my breath caught in my throat, I peered out of my window and saw the ambulance tearing down my driveway. But it didn't stop at my house. It kept going toward Ruthie's.

I jumped out of bed and ran to the back door. What if something had happened to her? We hadn't spoken since that day in the woods three weeks ago. She said she hated me and made no attempt to prove otherwise. There were no knowing glances between us and no secret meetings in the library. Only cold stares or complete ambivalence. I tried to pretend it didn't bother me. I tried to pretend that my time with Ruthie was just a phase I would grow out of. But deep down, I knew it was more.

Leaves crunched beneath my bare feet as I ran toward her cottage. When I got there, they were loading a gurney onto the ambulance. The body on it was covered with a sheet - a sure sign of death. I think my heart momentarily stopped.

"Sorry for your loss, Ruthie," someone said.

I turned and saw her sitting on the steps in front of her house. I could breathe again.

Ruthie nodded numbly while staring straight ahead. She seemed frozen in place as the ambulance slowly made its way down the hill toward the main road.

I stared at her in silence for a moment. I wanted to hold her. I wanted to reach out and stroke her curly brown hair. But I wasn't sure if I could, knowing what I knew. I wasn't sure if she would let me.

Slowly, forcing one foot at a time to move, I walked toward the porch. I sat next to her on the steps, the way I used to do when we were children. I remembered the countless times she had doctored my wounds there. She always took care of me. Now it was my turn to take care of her and I couldn't.

"My grandmother's dead," she said after a few moments, still staring into space.

"I know." I lifted my hand to place it on her shoulder and paused. I put my hand back on my leg. How was a brother supposed to touch his sister? I didn't know. I thought it best not to touch her at all.

We sat in silence as I racked my brain, trying to figure out a way to comfort her. There was nothing I could say. Nothing I could do but sit there. Hopefully, that was enough to let her know that I would always be there for her.

"It's true, isn't it?" she said finally.

"What is?"

"He's my father."

I closed my eyes tightly to hold back the tears that instantly formed. I nodded.

"Last week my grandmother started coughing and didn't stop. I knew she was going to die. I started going through all the documents I could find, trying to figure out –"

She stopped abruptly and put her head in her hands. Then she took a deep breath and said, "He's my legal guardian. Always has been." She lifted her head at stared at the same spot of nothingness. "Why in the world would he want custody of a little nigger girl unless I was *his* little nigger girl?"

"Ruthie, don't talk like that."

She stood and turned toward me. "Why not? Why the hell not? What does it matter? What am I supposed to do, Stephen?"

I stood as well and reached for her. She spun away from me.

"I feel like I'm trapped in some sort of nightmare and I can't wake up," she said, digging her fingers into her scalp. "Just tell me this isn't real. Tell me we're not brother and sister. Tell me I'm not completely alone in the world. Tell me you love me and we'll be together forever."

I folded her into my arms and let her cry on my chest. I couldn't tell her any of that. I did love her, but what good would it have done to tell her that?

\*\*\*

"I've asked Ruthie to move in with us," my father said the next night at dinner.

I was too stunned to respond, so I just stared at him.

"She's my daughter and she should be with her family," he continued. "She should be with me, her father. There's no need for her to live alone in that cottage."

I couldn't believe the words coming out of his mouth. Was he completely delusional? What was all this talk about family?

"She can stay in Matthew's old room."

My stomach knotted. This situation was getting more and more twisted. How was I supposed to live in the same house with the woman I loved, who also happened to be my sister? Not only that, but she was to sleep in my dead brother's room?

"How can you be so insensitive?" I heard the words spoken in my own voice, but somehow I didn't recognize that I had said them until I saw my father's face.

I couldn't think of a worse torture. It was bad enough knowing she was just a short walk away at her cottage. Having her in the same house with me, with just a wall separating us, would be unbearable.

Thankfully, my mother sensed my anxiety.

"What will people think?" she said, not lifting her eyes from her plate.

Was it possible that my father hadn't even considered the scandal this would cause? My father opened his mouth to dispute my mother, but nothing came out. Instead, he silently left the table and went to his room. That was the last we heard of that idea.

"You have a phone call," my mother said a week later as I was lying in bed. I thought maybe it was Julius wanting to get together to play ball or something.

"I'm not here." I wasn't ready to reenter the world yet. It had been a month since my disastrous attempt to go back to school. I was probably flunking out. I didn't care. I knew my father would figure out some way to force my teachers to pass me. I had spent so much of the past two months in bed that I had forgotten how to interact with people. I hadn't even seen my parents since my father's ridiculous request to let Ruthie move in with us a week ago. I was falling apart.

"It sounds important," she continued.

"Take a message." My mother hesitated a moment, trying to figure out something to say to get me out of bed. Apparently, nothing came to her because she just turned around and left. A few minutes later she came back.

"He won't leave a message. He says he really needs to talk to you." Annoyed, I threw my blanket off and tossed my legs over the side of the bed. It took more energy than I thought and I fell back down. My mother reached out to steady me, but I swatted her arm away. I felt lightheaded and dizzy from too much sleep and not enough food. I had to brace myself on my dresser for a while before I had the strength to make it all the way to the living room to pick up the phone.

"What," I said flatly when I finally made it.

"Stephen, you need to get down to Paul Morrison's house now." I couldn't believe Julius had gotten me out of bed to invite me to a party. Was that what was so important? And a party at Paul's house, no less. I hated that guy. I couldn't think of one reason why I would ever need to step foot in his house.

"Julius, I'm sick. I think I'm gettin' the flu or somethin'. Maybe next weekend -"

"It's Ruthie," he interrupted me. "Get here, now."

# Chapter 20

I dropped the phone and looked for my keys. I hadn't driven anywhere in weeks so I had no idea where they could be. I finally found them on top of the refrigerator and dashed out the door. It wasn't until I was sitting behind the wheel that I realized I wasn't wearing a shirt, but I didn't care. Ruthie was in trouble. She needed me.

When I got to Paul's house, Julius was waiting for me on the curb.

"What took you so long?"

"Where is she? What's wrong?"

"Damn, Stephen, what happened to you?" he asked when he saw the bruises on my chest.

"I said, 'where is she?'" I grabbed Julius by the collar. I was losing my patience with him. If Ruthie was in trouble, I didn't want to waste time with irrelevant questions.

"Calm down. She's inside."

"What's wrong with her?"

"She's drunk. She's not acting like herself. I was afraid something might happen to her." I let go of him and looked around. There were cars everywhere. It was one of Paul's famous parties that usually ended with a police raid and several people going to jail on possession charges. This was not Ruthie's type of party. How did she get involved with these people?

"She wouldn't listen to me. That girl has a wild side I never knew about," Julius said. I gave him a fierce look before he went any further. I didn't want to know the details of what she had done tonight.

I was marching up towards the front door, intent on taking Ruthie home, when Julius grabbed my arm. "Wait a minute, Stephen. You can't just go barging in there like some sort of barbarian, throw her over your shoulder and run out. You gotta play it cool. Here, take my jacket." I put on his jacket and flipped up the collar. I ran my fingers through my hair and tried to calm down. It didn't really matter, though. When I got inside the house, most of the people were passed out. The rest were too drunk to pay much attention to me.

The house was completely trashed and smelled of beer and vomit. Paul was fairly wealthy, so it struck me as odd that he would let people destroy his house like this. But I really didn't care about Paul or his house right now. I had to find Ruthie. I made my way through the living room, the den, the kitchen, stepping over bottles, cans and people -- still no sign of her. Julius and I started opening bedroom doors and glancing in, but I was really hoping not to find her in any of them. Behind each door was a progressively worse scenario: rooms filled with smoke or beds filled with naked bodies. It took only a few seconds to determine that Ruthie wasn't in any of these rooms. Most of the occupants were white. The only black people I'd seen at the party at all were Julius, Anthony Everson, and three black girls whose names I couldn't think of.

After circling the house three times, Julius wanted to give up.

"Maybe she caught a ride home," he said.

"I have to be sure." I headed outside toward my truck. I saw Ruthie down the street, making out with Bruce Connelly against his car. My heart raced and ached. I knew she had to move on. Would I ever get used to seeing her with other men?

Ruthie got into Bruce's car and they drove off. I don't know why, but I followed them.

They ended up at his house. I watched as he opened her car door and then led her to front door of his house. Once inside, he turned on some music and they started slow dancing in his living room.

I was so jealous of him. I wanted to be the one dancing with her. They started kissing and I had to hold myself back. I wanted to go in there and get him away from her. But that wasn't my job. She had chosen to go out with him and she obviously liked him.

137

He didn't kiss her the way I did. He didn't gently savor every soft curve of her lips. His kisses were hard and crude. He was increasingly rougher with her. It almost looked like he was trying to force her to go further. Ruthie must have gotten the same impression because she pulled away from him. It looked like she was trying to explain something to him, like she didn't want to kiss anymore, but he didn't listen to her and started to kiss her again. This time when she pulled away he slapped her across the face. I jumped out of my truck as fast as I could and ran to the house. The door was locked. I could hear Ruthie screaming inside, but I couldn't get in. Finally, I punched through the glass in the door and unlocked it from the inside. By the time I reached the living room, Bruce had ripped her shirt open and was lying on top of her, trying to remove her panties. I pulled him off of her and threw him across the room.

"Stephen? What the --" I punched him in the face. He staggered back, then touched his mouth as if he couldn't believe he was bleeding.

"Come on, Stephen. You had your chance with her; now it's time to share." I lost control. I tackled him and we crashed into his coffee table. I don't know how many times I hit him. He went unconscious, but I just kept beating him. In my mind, his face turned into my father's. I could have killed him. I thought I was going to, but I heard Ruthie pleading with me to stop.

I turned around and she was quivering in the corner, clutching her ripped blouse to her chest. I went over to pick her up and she jerked away from me. At first, she wouldn't let me touch her.

"Ruthie, it's okay. I'm not gonna hurt you." I kissed her forehead and stroked her hair. She stared into my eyes for a moment as if she was trying to remember who I was. Finally, she put her arms around my neck and I carried her to my truck.

She fell asleep in my lap on the way to her house. When we got there, I picked her up and carried her to her bed. Tears burned my eyes as I thought of the things we had done in that very bed...and how much I still wanted to do those things.

I laid her in the bed and turned to leave. I had to get out of there as soon as possible. I didn't know if I could resist the burning desire I had for her.

"Stephen," she called softly, just as I reached to door to the hallway.

I let my head fall against the frame. "Yes?"

"Don't leave me alone. I can't be alone tonight."

I didn't respond. I couldn't.

"Stephen, please."

I closed my eyes and took a deep breath. I tried to push every romantic or sexual thought out of my mind. Over and over I repeated the phrase, "She's my sister."

"Okay," I said, when I felt like I had control.

I went over to the bed, covered her with the blanket and then sat down rigidly. She reached for me. "Hold me, Stephen."

I didn't want to, but how could I deny her comfort after what she'd been through tonight?

I inched closer, then lifted her and held her against my chest. Our breathing synced; our chests rose and fell in unison. We stayed like that for so long that I thought she'd fallen asleep. But I was wrong.

"I love you, Stephen," she said into my chest.

I didn't respond.

"And not like a sister loves her brother. I love you like a woman loves her man. I love you with the overwhelming, blinding passion of a thousand suns."

Why was she telling me this?

"Don't do this, Ruthie. Don't make this any harder than it already is. We can't be together."

"Why not?" She sat up and looked at me. "This isn't our fault. We didn't choose this. Why should we be punished for the mistakes of our parents?"

"Ruthie, we –"

"Make love to me, Stephen."

"What?" I jumped off the bed, needing to put as much distance as possible between us.

"If we do it once knowing the truth, it will get easier after that. Soon it won't matter at all. Because it doesn't. It doesn't matter."

She had a possessed look in her eyes as she stood up and followed me. Did she really believe what she was saying?

My body erupted in flames when she kissed me. It had been too long. She started ripping off my clothes and guided me toward the bed.

"Make love to me, Stephen. Please."

Maybe she was right. Maybe it didn't matter. No one else had to know.

"Oh, Ruthie. I love you. I love you. I love you," I said, trying to make up for the weeks I hadn't allowed myself to say it out loud.

We undressed each other feverishly. Soon were completely naked on the bed. Caressing. Rubbing. But then, as if on cue, we stopped and turned away from each other. Ruthie started crying. We couldn't do it. Not now that we knew the truth.

I grabbed what I could find of my clothes and went to sleep on the couch.

## Chapter 21

Sometime before dawn I forced my eyelids open and saw Ruthie sitting at the end of the couch. Without saying a word, she handed me a cup of coffee.

"I'm sorry about last night," she said after I'd taken a few sips.

"You don't have to apologize."

She stared down at her hands. "I shouldn't have gone to Bruce's house. I shouldn't have forced myself on you like that. I don't know what I was thinking."

"It's not your fault."

We fell into silence. The sun peeked through the yellow curtains of her living room. I needed to get home soon, before Father realized I was gone.

"Let me see your hand," she said when I'd finished my coffee. Her voice was barely a whisper, as if she was trying to hold back an onslaught of tears. At first I wondered why she wanted my hand, but then I remembered that I'd punched through a glass window the night before. My hand was swollen and encrusted with dried blood. She took some tweezers and tried to get out all the remnants of glass before she cleaned the cuts and scrapes. I just stared at her the entire time. There she was, taking care of me again. I was glad I had been there for her last night when she needed me. It was nice to return the favor, for once.

"I couldn't get it all. You may want to get some stitches or take some medicine so it won't get infected," she said as she wrapped my hand with gauze and kissed it. I caressed her face with my other hand, just relishing the opportunity to touch her, to spend time with her. She closed her eyes tightly and leaned into my touch. "I can't take this anymore."

I dropped my hand and turned away. I knew what she meant. Seeing each other nearly every day and not being able to be together was slowly killing us.

"I'm going back to New York."

I took a deep breath. "When?" I couldn't fight her. I couldn't beg her to stay. I just had to accept it.

She shrugged. "Today, I guess. Nothing is keeping me here. I have no reason to stay."

"Where will you live?"

She sighed. "A girl from the art school said I could stay with her for a while." Ruthie stood up and hugged herself. "I've been thinking about it for a few weeks, actually. I'll live with Marie; maybe get a job as a waitress or something while I try to sell some of my work."

I nodded. It was as good a plan as any. "Can I give you some money?" I asked, looking toward the window again. "I've been saving since..." I couldn't finish the sentence. I'd been saving money ever since our first kiss by the lake.

"No, I'm okay. Grandma Esther had some money saved."

The silence crashed upon us. I stood and slipped my feet into my sneakers. After throwing on my coat, I headed for the door. "Do you need anything?" I asked, my hand resting on the doorknob. Part of me wanted her to say she needed *me*. But what good would that have done? We needed to end this torment. Putting a few states between us was probably the most logical thing to do.

"Just a ride to the bus station," she said.

I nodded. "I'll pick you up in two hours?"

"Okay."

# Chapter 22

"So, Ruthie moved back to New York and you stayed in Virginia?" Lt. Drake asked

I nodded.

Lt. Drake looked at his watch. "It's almost five a.m. Why don't I get us some caffeine?"

I nodded again then started rubbing the soreness out of my neck muscles as Lt. Drake left the room in search of drinks. I was beyond exhausted. Ruthie and I hadn't slept much during the four days we were on the run. And sitting in the same place all night, rehashing my turbulent life, added to my emotional fatigue.

Lt. Drake returned and placed a bottle of soda and a stale donut in front of me.

"Thanks," I said, before biting into it. I was so hungry I would've eaten anything. I wondered if Ruthie had been given more in the way of sustenance than me.

"Is Ruthie okay?" I asked.

"Yeah, she's fine. She's asleep in a holding cell."

"She's in a cell?" I nearly choked on a crumb of donut. They were treating her like a criminal.

"Relax; she's not under arrest or anything. She's just using the bed to get some sleep."

I sighed in relief. I was glad she was getting the much-needed rest, but I missed her.

"Can I see her?"

Lt. Drake rubbed his chin. "I don't know -"

"Please?"

He sighed. "Alright, I'll make you a deal. I'll take you to see her, but I'm going to have to handcuff you again. I can't take a chance that you might run off before we finish this interview."

"That's fine." I set my soda down and held out my hands.

After he secured the cuffs to my wrists, Lt. Drake led me down a narrow hallway, past several cells holding miscellaneous drunks and prostitutes. I hoped Ruthie hadn't been forced into their company.

Thankfully, Ruthie was resting in an otherwise empty cell. She was fast asleep on a cot in the middle of the room. Her brown curls were piled in a messy knot on the side of her face. Her right arm hung limply over the edge of the cot. She looked beautiful. I wanted to go in and kiss her, but I knew that wasn't going to happen. Before I knew it, we were heading back to the interrogation room.

"You know, I was thinking about something," Lt. Drake said as we walked back. "When you were a kid,

Matthew bought you and Ruthie a dog, didn't he? I don't think you said anything about her since you told me about looking for Matthew's body. What happened to the dog?"

I sat down in the familiar wooden chair as Lt. Drake unlocked my handcuffs. "I tried to block that night out of my memory," I said as he sat across from me. I sighed. "One afternoon when I was eleven, my dad was taking a nap. He had been up most of the night giving last rites to one of his church members. Goldie started barking. Without saying a word, he came out of his room, grabbed his shotgun, and shot her in the backyard."

Lt. Drake's eyes widened. I could tell he was an animal lover.

He cleared his throat. "Where was Ruthie?"

"She was at the grocery store with her grandmother. I buried Goldie and made sure there was no sign of her when Ruthie came back." I had to pause and hold in the tears. "I never got to grieve for Goldie. If I cried, Ruthie would've wondered why and I didn't want her to know. I told her that Goldie ran away."

Lt. Drake shook his head as if trying to shake the image of my dead dog out of his mind. "So, let me get this straight so far." He leaned forward. "You and Ruthie are brother and sister; you can't stay away from each other so Ruthie decides to move away."

I nodded.

"How long was she gone?" he asked.

"Two years."

"How did you handle it?"

"Not well. It was a dark time in my life. I didn't like what I turned into. I did a lot of drugs. I don't even remember some of the awful things I did to people. But I'll fill you in on what I do remember."

# Chapter 23

Two weeks after Ruthie left, Julius and I were playing basketball in silence. It wasn't a real game; we were just shooting around in the school gym. He could tell I didn't want to talk, but after a while his curiosity got the best of him.

"Alright, are you going to tell me what's going on with you?" he asked.

"What do you mean?" I responded casually as I took another shot. I didn't know whether I was ready to talk about the situation yet, or not.

"I mean, what's up with all those bruises on your chest? Did you get in another fight or somethin'?" I had forgotten that he'd seen me without my shirt the night I'd rescued Ruthie from Bruce two weeks ago.

"Yeah, something like that." I missed the shot, but it bounced right back to me so I took another shot. This time Julius got the rebound.

"Well, who was it? I can help you take him out."

I didn't answer as Julius took his shot. He sighed, annoyed with my reluctance to elaborate.

"You used to be this hip genius that everyone liked and now you're just...I don't know...you're different. What happened?"

I still didn't say anything. I felt myself losing it. I didn't know how many more of his questions I could take.

"And what's up with you and Ruthie? I thought you guys were together. Why was she at that party with Bruce? Did you break up or somethin'?"

"Yeah, something like that," I said as I tried to get the ball after he took another shot, but Julius beat me to it.

"Well, where is she? I haven't seen her in like, two weeks. If she's on the market let me know so I can tell Timothy. He's so into that girl it's ridiculous. Just promise you won't beat him up," he said only halfway joking. That did it. I walked over to the bench and started packing up my stuff.

"Whoa, hey, what'd I say?"

I just ignored him. I didn't feel like explaining myself and I didn't feel like hearing about what guys were "into" my Ruthie.

"What is up with you, man?" He wasn't joking anymore. He really wanted to know what was going on. "You been actin' strange for months now. If you ain't pickin' fights with random guys, you're holed up in your room and I

don't see you for days. Just tell me. It can't be that bad. Did you get her pregnant or something? I can help you out with –
"

"She's my sister," I said quietly. I don't know what made me say it. But once it was out, it was kind of a relief. Julius looked at me sideways, then he started to smile.

"I'm serious, man." he said, tossing the ball to me playfully.

"I'm serious, too. Why would I lie about that?"

"Whoa, that's messed up," he said when he saw that I wasn't kidding.

"My father is her father. Now you know. Are you happy now?" I threw the ball back at him, forcefully. He caught it, but it threw him off balance a little.

"Did you guys...you know...?"

"Yeah. A lot."

"Whoa, that's messed up."

"Will you stop saying that?"

"Well, what am I supposed to say?"

"I don't know," I said. Julius sat next to me on the bench and we both just stared into space for a while.

"Does she know?"

"Yeah."

"Whoa, that's...I mean. Sorry." Julius dribbled the ball slowly. I could tell he was uncomfortable and trying to find the right thing to say. "So, since you can't have her, you've been beatin' up every guy that gets close to her," he said.

I didn't answer.

"You still love her, don't you?" he asked after a while.

"That's irrelevant."

"No, it ain't."

"What do you mean?"

"No one else knows and no one else has gotta know. I won't tell. Just move away together."

"That's disgusting."

"Hey, I'm just sayin' if you wanna be together, go ahead and do it. Who's gonna think you're related?"

"That's not an option," I said as I grabbed my stuff and started walking out of the gym.

"Fine, just keep flyin' off the handle every time you see her with someone. That's a great solution, Stephen. You know everyone thinks you've lost your mind!"

"Well, I don't have to worry about beating up other guys anymore because she's gone."

Julius ran to catch up with me at the door. "What do you mean, she's gone?"

"She went back to New York."

"Oh..." He started dribbling the ball again. It was his way of thinking. "Look, man," he said after a few seconds, "I know you might think it's gross now, but just think about going after her and being with her. No one else would know. As long as she didn't get pregnant...no problem."

I tried to think about it. I really did. So many times I wanted to just hop in my truck and drive to New York to find her. But I couldn't. How were we supposed to have a happy life together with that secret between us? It wasn't possible. It was time for me to move on and find someone else.

***

"Stephen? Stephen, are you listening to me?" Mary Elizabeth was trying to get my attention. She had been talking nonstop for twenty minutes about her weekend shopping trip in New York with her parents. I was lying on her bed as she showed me purchase after purchase. It just reminded me of Ruthie. I wondered what she was doing, how she was surviving in that big city, all alone. I wanted to be there for her. I felt a pain in my chest. It hurt to swallow. I closed my eyes and tried to block out Mary Elizabeth's words.

Two months earlier I had called her, out of the blue, and asked her for a date. We'd been together ever since. In order to tolerate her, I'd mastered the art of tuning out her constant chatter. She quickly picked up on the lack of attention I was giving her fashion show.

"Why do I always feel like when you're with me, you're really somewhere else?"

"What are you talking about? I'm right here." I did the boyfriendly thing. I grabbed her hand and pulled her next to me on the bed. I tried to caress her cheek, but she turned away from me.

"I was so excited when you asked me out. It was like a dream. I thought that we could actually have a future together." She wasn't looking at me, but I could tell she was starting to cry.

"We can." I lied.

"Don't be ridiculous, Stephen. You're in my room, lying on my bed. I've been parading around you half-naked for half an hour and it's like I'm not even here."

"What are you talking about?" Just then I noticed that she had been changing in and out of outfits the entire time. She was now wearing just her bra, panties, and a frilly pink skirt. I guess it didn't have the effect she wanted.

"I wanted you to be my first," she sobbed. She wanted to have sex with me? I hadn't even thought about it with her.

I was completely taken aback. I went to hug her and tried to kiss her neck, but she stood up.

"Oh, forget it, Stephen. Stop pretending that you could ever love me as much as I love you. It's not fair to either one of us."

"Mary Elizabeth, I do…"

"Don't lie to me, please. Just leave and let me preserve a little of my dignity." She turned her back to me and looked out the window, furiously wiping tears from her face.

I got off the bed and stood behind her. I lifted her hair and tenderly kissed the back of her neck. I lied to her. I told her exactly what she wanted to hear. Then I unsnapped her bra and laid her down. My mouth covered her breasts. I massaged her nipples with my tongue while my fingers slipped into her panties. I can't say what we did next was making love. It was just sex. I could never love her, which is why I never called her again after that day.

Taking an innocent girl's virginity to fill my own selfish needs should have made me feel guilty. It didn't, though. I just felt empty, alone, numb. No guilt whatsoever, which is why I continued to do it. I went from one girl to the next, somehow making each of them believe that they were the most special thing in my life. Like I said before, I had a talent for making people see only what I wanted them to see.

After I went through all the white girls in town, I moved on to the black girls. In particular, Rosalee Hines, one of Ruthie's friends, held a certain attraction. Rosalee and I would go to the fanciest restaurants and I would cause a scene as often as I could. If they so much as failed to fill up our water glasses in a timely fashion, I would accuse the entire restaurant of being racist. I don't know whether I

157

really liked Rosalee or whether I just wanted to embarrass my father.

It was 1974 and while interracial dating wasn't exactly accepted in Livingston, it happened often enough, as evidenced by the few children in town who were too black to be white and too white to be black. I should have recognized that Ruthie fell into that category. I think a part of me had been in denial all my life. As long as no one spoke about mixed-race affairs or brought too much attention to the practice, people could pretend it didn't exist.

I thought cavorting in public with Negro women would anger my father. But as it turns out, he really didn't care what I did. He only cared about one thing.

"Have you heard from Ruth?" he asked one night, before one of my dates with Rosalee.

I couldn't believe he had the audacity to ask me about her. How could he even mention her name in front of me? I had just gotten to the point where I didn't have to remind myself not to think about her. I could finally kiss a woman and not compare her to my sister. My wounds were starting to heal. Now he had to go and open the wound again with just the mention of her name. That's when it hit me. My father was hurting, too. In his own sick way, he loved his daughter. He loved her more than he ever loved me.

I shook my head. My father stared down into his glass of scotch, then shuffled to his bedroom. I left the house to go pick up Rosalee.

After dinner, I took her to a popular make-out spot on the outskirts of town. It was a romantic place up in the mountains where I often brought girls when I wanted to get high or have sex. There was even a name for it, something like 'Make-Out Point' or 'Hot Spot Hill', or something stupid like that.

"You're so beautiful." I said between kisses as I unbuttoned her blouse. I wasn't completely lying. She was cute with her ebony complexion and huge, gorgeous, white smile, but I don't think I was thinking about her that night, which was proven by what I said next.

"I love you, Ruthie."

"What did you say?" Rosalee quickly pulled away from me.

"What? I said I love you."

"What did you call me?"

"Rosie. I called you Rosie." For a moment I honestly believed I did say Rosie instead of Ruthie.

"The hell you did. You called me Ruthie. Again."

"No, I didn't. And what do you mean 'again'? I've never called you Ruthie."

"Last week, at that French restaurant, you called me Ruthie." She was getting angry. She was already buttoning

159

her shirt and simultaneously getting out of the truck. She had every right to be angry. I knew what I had done. I didn't know why I did it. She didn't look like Ruthie. She didn't smell like her, feel like her, or taste like her. No one did. No one could replace my Ruthie. But I was doomed to spend the rest of my life searching for someone to fall in love with that reminded me enough of my sister.

"Rosalee, I'm sorry. I didn't mean it. Get back in the truck."

"Look, if you're so in love with Ruthie then be with her. Don't mess around with me." I wish it were that easy. She had no idea how much I wanted it to be that way. It frustrated me the way she treated the situation so nonchalantly.

"You should just shut the hell up about things you know nothing about!" I yelled at her. Something in my voice really scared her. She started backing away from the truck.

"Just stay away from me," she said.

I was turning into some sort of monster and I knew it. I had to get myself together. Somehow I convinced her to get back in the truck and I drove her home. The next day she dumped me. I can't say I blame her.

I continued in this cycle of sabotaging relationships and alienating myself from every other human being until about a week ago. Then everything changed.

# Chapter 24

It wasn't coincidence; it was fate that led me to the town's ice cream parlor last week. It was the same place Matthew used to take us when we were kids. For some reason, I couldn't get Matthew or Ruthie out of my mind that day. I sat in a window seat and let my sundae melt as I stared out the window, watching the street. That's when I saw her.

After two years, my Ruthie looked exactly the same. Her brown hair had been straightened and it hung down her back. She almost glowed in the yellow sundress she wore. With her friends, Rosalee and Adelaide, on either side of her, she laughed and giggled as they entered the dress shop across the street.

I was so mesmerized by the sight of her, I don't even remember leaving the ice cream parlor and crossing Main Street. But moments later, I stood in front of the dress shop as Ruthie exited.

She froze in front of me. We stared at each other in silence for an eternity. My heart felt like it was in my throat.

Finally, Rosalee said, "Ruthie, we're going on to the pharmacy. You can catch up with us there." Then she pulled

Adelaide away, leaving Ruthie and me alone. I thought I sensed a little hostility from Rosalee. We didn't exactly end on a good note.

"Hi." I don't remember which one of us said it, but the isolated salutation just hung in the air for several seconds.

"Adelaide is getting married this weekend," she said finally. "A Fourth of July wedding. She wanted me to be a bridesmaid."

I nodded. That explained why she was in town. But it didn't explain why she hadn't contacted me. That's what I really wanted to know.

For two years I had thought about what I'd say if I saw her again. I constantly replayed possible conversations in my head. But in that moment, nothing came to me.

"How are you?" I said, resorting to polite conversation.

"I'm fine. You?"

I nodded. I wasn't quite sure what to say. I knew I didn't want to tell her that I really wasn't fine. That my life had crumbled and I'd turned into a shell of my former self that rarely left the house. I'd basically turned into my mother.

"Are you growing a beard?" she asked, touching my chin.

I covered her hand with mine. "I just haven't felt like shaving in a few days."

She smiled slightly, then she jerked her hand away and shoved it into her pocket as if suddenly remembering where she was. She looked around self-consciously.

"I miss you," I blurted. It wasn't the wisest thing for me to say, but I couldn't hold it in. It just came out.

Ruthie turned away and started blinking rapidly. She was holding back tears. In that moment, I knew she missed me, too.

By the time I got home that afternoon, my father already knew Ruthie was in town.

"Do you think she'll join us for dinner?" he said to no one in particular as he paced the living room. He downed the Scotch in his hand, then reached for another.

"Who?" I knew exactly who he was talking about. I think I just felt like being obstinate.

"Mabel." He shut his eyes and held the glass of ice to his forehead. "Ruthie. I mean Ruthie."

"I highly doubt she will ever step foot in this house again," I said through gritted teeth as I stormed off to my room.

"Well, why on Earth not? I'm her father," he said from the other room. He had completely lost his grip on reality. Did he think he could have a real father-daughter relationship with her?

After I lay down in bed, I heard my father leave the house. I wondered if he was going to search out Ruthie and invite her to dinner. I knew she wouldn't come. I knew she would stay as far away from this house as possible. But a part of me wished she would come over. I longed to see her again. Though the sight of her was painful, it also filled a crushing void inside of me. Being around her again would be exquisite torment.

I fell asleep to memories of our time together. For some reason, I didn't feel the shame that I should have.

What felt like seconds later, I heard an unexpected sound -- the doorbell. We never had visitors. I couldn't remember the last time I heard someone use our doorbell. It rang several more times before I finally dragged myself out of bed in order to answer it.

When I swung open the door, I thought I was staring at a ghost. "Matthew?"

# Chapter 25

"What's up, little brother?" he said, reaching out to hug me.

I was so shocked I couldn't respond. I hugged him back firmly, afraid that if I let go he might disappear. I didn't know how it was that fate brought Ruthie and Matthew back into my life on the same day, but I didn't question it. I just held on to my older brother.

"I've been outside for a few hours, but I didn't want to come in until Theodore left," he said, pulling away.

I just stared at him with my mouth open.

"Stephen, what's wrong?"

"I...I...I thought you were dead."

"Dead? Is that what he told you?"

I thought back to that day thirteen years ago when he disappeared. I had concentrate in order to remember what my father actually said.

"No, he said you joined the Navy." I took a step back and looked at him. He didn't look like he was in the Navy. He was scruffy and unshaven. His long, stringy hair would definitely not have been permitted in the military. He was wearing a long tie-dyed shirt - the kind that hippies wore in the 60's - and tattered jeans.

"The Navy, huh? Well, that's creative."

"Where have you been?"

"I was -"

"Who's there?" My mother asked as she walked into the living room, rubbing her eyes. She had been in one of her comatose sleeps, even though it was only 5:00 in the evening. She took advantage of the fact that my father was out of the house. Anytime he was there, he would work her like a slave. She needed the rest. When she saw Matthew, she stopped dead in her tracks.

"Oh, Matthew!" she cried as she ran into his arms. He picked her up and swung her around. I hadn't seen her this happy in years. In fact, I hadn't seen her this happy since Matthew left thirteen years ago.

"I missed you so much," they said simultaneously. They started talking fast, firing questions back and forth. What are you doing here? How are you? Are you all right? Is he treating you any better? Why did you cut your hair? Do you still have that bracelet I gave you?

"Where's your luggage?" I interrupted. They both looked at me.

"I'm staying at a motel.  Didn't want to be a burden."
What he meant to say was that he didn't want to stay under
the same roof as our father.  I can't say I blame him for that.

"Stephen, go get Matthew a drink."  I knew she was
just trying to get rid of me, so I pretended to comply.

"What's going on here?" he said when he thought
they were alone.  "You two look horrible.  What has he done
to you?  Why is Stephen so thin and pale?"

"He's been through a lot, recently. He and Ruthie fell
in love and ..." My mother started sobbing.

"Good God, no one told them Theodore was Ruthie's
father?"  he said as he held her and kissed the top of her head,
trying to console her.  Matthew knew, too?  How is it that
everyone knew but me? Or maybe I just didn't want to know.
I had ignored all the signs.

As I watched Matthew hold my mother, *our* mother,
something inside me shivered.  They way he looked at her,
the way he touched her, the way they looked standing next to
each other...I don't know.   There was just some unsaid
connection between them that I had never noticed before.
"You have to get out of here," Matthew said.  "Come with me
to Phoenix.  Both of you.  I have a place out there."

"You know I can't do that."

"I'll protect you.  I swear I'll kill him if he touches
you again.  I've thought of you and Stephen every day for

thirteen years. I couldn't stay away any longer. I don't care what he does to me; we just have to get you out of here."

Thirteen years. Matthew disappeared thirteen years ago, when he was twenty-two. That would make him thirty-five years old right now. I didn't know how old my mother was when she had him, but she would at least have to be fifty years old right now, right? I took another look at my mother and brother. Somehow, both of them looked forty. How was that possible? Maybe my mother just looked young for her age and Matthew looked old for his. But I would think with all the abuse my mother endured, she would be the one to look older than her true age. I was completely confused.

"There's something I have to tell you," my mother said as she wiped tears away from her sad, yet still youthful, face.

"What?"

"Not here. Where are you staying? You better go before he gets home. I don't want any problems." Matthew scribbled something down on a sheet of paper, gave my mother a long hug, and scrambled out the door.

# Chapter 26

The next day was Adelaide's wedding. She was marrying Julius's brother, Timothy, so I had been invited. But I had never considered actually going until I found out Ruthie was in the wedding. I knew she would look beautiful. I had to see her again.

As I was straightening my tie, my mother poked her head in my room. "I need you to take me somewhere," she said.

I stared at her in a moment of confusion. My mother wanted to leave the house? The only time she ever left the house was for church or social events mandated by my father. Where was she going on a Saturday afternoon, and without my father?

"I have to talk to Matthew," she said, as if perceiving my confusion. "I need you to take me to his motel."

Mentioning Matthew brought back another question of mine.

"Mother, how old are you?"

She turned away and rubbed her neck. "You're never supposed to ask a lady her age," she said, trying to make a joke.

"Mother, I need the truth. There are too many secrets in this family."

She sighed. "Okay, if you must know -- I'm thirty-eight."

"What?" I said, a little more forcefully than I meant to.

My mother covered her head and cowered as if she believed I would hit her.

"I'm sorry. I didn't mean to yell," I said softly as I put my hand on her back. Her reaction brought tears to my eyes. How could she ever think I would strike her? I rubbed her back for a moment, then slowly folded her into a hug. She cried into my chest.

I took a deep breath before saying, "Okay, so you're not Matthew's mother. It's not possible. He's thirty-five and you're thirty-eight." I don't know how I didn't pick up their ages before. How did I not notice that they were practically the same age? But then again, I was only five when he left. At that age, all I knew was that she was my mother and Matthew was my brother. I just assumed she was his mother too.

"So Theodore is Matthew's father, my father, and Ruthie's father. But we all have different mothers." I said by way of summary. I was still trying to wrap my head around everything. The realization of our parentage made me hate my father even more. He'd had three children by three different women, yet he led a congregation as if he had some sort of moral authority. What's more, he took no responsibility for his actions. He blamed Ruthie's mother for forcing him to stray. I wondered what the story with Matthew's mother was.

"What happened to Matthew's mother? Was Theodore married before you?" I asked.

My mother shook her head. "I'll tell you everything. I promise. I just need to speak to Matthew first."

After dropping off my mother, I found myself sitting in Livingston's only predominantly black church. Standing next to his brother at the altar, Julius gave me a shocked look. He was surprised to see me, considering I had barely left my house in months. After the shock wore off, he smiled and gave me a wave.

When the music started, Ruthie was the first to walk down the aisle. The sight of her paralyzed me. I couldn't take my eyes off of her. I bet Ruthie had convinced Adelaide to make the bridesmaid's dresses yellow. Ruthie always looked amazing in yellow -- today was no exception. Even when the music changed and everyone stood up to get a better look at the bride coming down the aisle, I continued to stare at Ruthie.

I made sure I chose a seat that would put me in Ruthie's direct line of sight as she stood at the altar. But she still did everything she could to avoid eye contact with me. She shifted her body to awkward angles as her eyes darted every which way except toward me.

Another bridesmaid leaned forward and whispered in Ruthie's ear, probably telling her to stop moving. Finally, Ruthie's gaze settled upon me. Once our eyes locked, they stayed that way for the rest of the ceremony. When the preacher said the words "man and wife," a tear spilled down Ruthie's cheek.

After the ceremony, I tried to get Ruthie alone so we could talk. I wanted to tell her about Matthew. She would be so excited to see him. But Ruthie had no intention of dredging up the past with me.

"Can we talk?" I asked, grabbing her arm outside the church.

"Let's not do this, Stephen. Let's not put ourselves through any more pain."

"But Ruthie, it's important."

She shook her head and pulled her arm free. "Let it go. Let us go." She ran down the four steps in front of the church and hopped into a station wagon with the other bridesmaids. A dust cloud bloomed behind it as it sped off down the dirt road. I knew it was headed to the old firehouse where the reception was being held. I never imagined myself attending an all-black wedding reception, but I had to go. I had to talk to Ruthie.

*** 

"I can't believe you actually came," Julius said, tackling me with a bear hug. "You're not the most social person."

"Yeah, well, I guess it's about time I start working on that."

Julius gave me a skeptical look, then followed my gaze across the room to where Ruthie was dancing with Adelaide's brother. "Yeah right. I know what you have on your mind. You're not gonna start another fight, are you?" he asked only half-joking.

I shook my head. "I'm past that. There's no hope for Ruthie and me. I know that now. I just want to talk to her."

Julius nodded while sipping his drink. The music changed to *Boogie Shoes* by K.C. and the Sunshine Band. Ruthie left her partner and headed toward the wedding party's table.

"Hey, how about I help you out. I'll go dance with her and in two minutes, you come and cut in."

Julius took a step away. I grabbed his arm and pulled him back. "You want me to dance? I can't dance."

He laughed. "That ain't my problem. It's your only hope. She's not going to cause a scene and refuse to dance with you. She wouldn't want to ruin Adelaide's party like that. So I suggest you put on your *boogie shoes* and cut in." Julius smiled at his little joke, then went to ask Ruthie for a dance.

My stomach stirred as I saw Julius lead Ruthie to the dance floor. I didn't know what made me more nervous, the fact that in a few moments I would be inches away from Ruthie or the fact that in a few moments everyone would be staring at the uncoordinated white boy. I did a quick scan of the party. Yep, I was the only white person. I closed my eyes and took a deep breath. It didn't matter, I was only doing this so I could have some alone time with Ruthie.

I strolled to the middle of the dance floor, trying to exude confidence. I barely tapped Julius on the shoulder once before he ducked out of the way, leaving Ruthie standing in front of me.

"Hi, Ruthie."

She sighed. "Stephen, I -"

"Let's dance," I said, cutting off whatever excuse she was about to formulate. I started hopping back and forth to the music, trying to imitate what Julius had been doing a moment before. From the smile that erupted across Ruthie's face I could tell I hadn't even come close.

Mercifully, the song ended after only a few more seconds. But then *These Arms of Mine* started playing, the song we first made love to.

Ruthie's eyes widened. She turned to leave, but I grabbed her arm and pulled her close to me. Her body was tense as I placed my hands on her waist. I buried my face in her hair and breathed in her scent. She smelled of vanilla, just like she had during our first kiss when we were only thirteen.

Slowly, she melted in my arms and returned my embrace. I wondered what she was thinking, but I wasn't brave enough to ask. I didn't want to ruin the moment. For just one song I wanted to pretend that everything was right in the world and that our love was acceptable. Even though it had been two years since I'd held her like this, I knew she still loved me. Two years wasn't enough time to break our connection.

"I thought I was over you," she said suddenly. "Every day for two years I woke up in the morning and told myself that what I felt for you was wrong. I tried to stamp out my feelings. I thought I had won. That's why I agreed to come back this weekend. I thought I was completely over you. But one look at you and everything came flooding back."

She still loved me! I couldn't respond. I thought I might start crying if I did. So instead, I just pulled her closer.

It wasn't until people started bumping into us while dancing to an Earth, Wind, and Fire song that either of us realized the Otis Redding song was over. Ruthie pulled away from me.

"I can never come back again. This is our last goodbye," she said before running off the dance floor.

I was paralyzed. I couldn't move. Then suddenly I remembered the real reason I wanted to talk to her. Matthew. I hadn't even brought up Matthew.

I ran after her and caught up with her in the parking lot.

"Ruthie, wait!"

"No, Stephen. I can't. This was a mistake. I shouldn't have come back."

I ran in front of her and blocked her path. "Matthew's alive!" I blurted before something else got in the way.

Ruthie crossed her arms and shook her head. "I can't believe you're resorting to using Matthew's name. That's pathetic, Stephen."

She tried to step around me, but I held her in place by grabbing her shoulders.

"I'm not resorting to anything. He's alive. I saw him with my own eyes."

"You'd say anything to get me to stay."

I sighed. "You're probably right. But you have to trust me, Ruthie. You know me. You know I wouldn't lie about something like this."

Ruthie studied my eyes, searching for the truth.

"You have to believe me. Don't you want to see him?"

She took a deep breath and let it out slowly. "I believe that you really believe this fantasy, which means you're worse off than I thought. You need help, Stephen."

"Fine, if it's a fantasy then come and prove it to me. Come show me how much help I need."

She sighed heavily. "Okay, let's go."

# Chapter 27

I knocked on Matthew's motel room door for a full five minutes. No one answered. My mother should have been there. I'd dropped her off at this very door right before the wedding. Ruthie stood next to me with her arms crossed and a smug look on her face. Her attitude might have really bothered me if I wasn't so worried about the whereabouts of my mother and Matthew. What if my father found out Matthew was in town?

I ran to the front office to see if I could find out any information.

"Excuse me, ma'am," I said to the woman behind the counter. "I'm looking for the guest in room six, Matthew Phillips; do you know when he left?"

The clerk picked up her clipboard and blew a bubble with her gum. "Ain't no Matthew Phillips in room six," she said.

Ruthie sighed and touched my arm. "Stephen, just give it up, okay?"

"There's a Matthew Clare in room six. He done left 'bout a hour ago wit some blonde woman."

"Matthew Clare?" I asked. I turned to Ruthie. "It's him. He must be using a fake name. And the blonde woman is my mother. I told you she was here with him."

Ruthie opened her mouth to dispute me, but before she could say anything I grabbed her hand and pulled her toward my truck.

"Something strange is going on," I told Ruthie as we drove to my house. I wasn't sure if Matthew and my mother had actually gone there, but I didn't know where else to start looking. "Do you know how old my mother is?"

Ruthie shrugged. "Forty-five? Fifty?"

"No, she's only thirty-eight."

Ruthie stared at me skeptically. "She can't be Matthew's mother."

"Exactly," I said. "She's not."

"How did we not notice that?"

I shrugged. "We were just kids."

"So, your...our...Theodore has three children from three different women?"

"Looks that way."

"What happened to Matthew's mother?"

"I don't know. But it has to have something to do with why my mother has stayed all these years. Maybe my father killed Matthew's mother and my mother was afraid he'd do the same to her."

Ruthie shivered at the thought and hugged herself.

180

"I'll wait in the car," Ruthie said when I pulled up to my house. "If Matthew is really in there, which I doubt, tell him to come out here."

I knew something was wrong before I even got out of the car. Matthew's Volkswagen van and my father's white Cadillac were both in the driveway, but the house was eerily quiet. There was no way the two of them could be in the same room without an immediate fight.

When I opened the door, I found the living room completely ransacked. There were handprints of blood on the walls. It smelled like...I don't know. Like nothing I'd ever smelled before. At first, I thought we had been robbed, but then I saw my mother sitting calmly on the couch. She was smiling. She never smiled. She had finally lost it, I thought.

"Mother, are you okay?"

"Twenty years. I'm free. I'm finally free." She laughed hysterically.

"Mother, where is Father?" I started to panic. I wasn't afraid that something had happened to him. I was just afraid that my mother had done it and that she would get in trouble.

"You don't have to call him Father anymore. He is not your father." She was acting so strangely I didn't know what to think. I knew I couldn't believe her. It would've

181

been a dream come true, though. But she was obviously out of her mind.

"And Matthew is not your brother." Now I knew she was crazy.

"Mother, what are you talking about? I think I need to take you to a doctor."

"No!" she screamed when I tried to touch her. "You need to hear this." She took my hand, pulled me down beside her and continued.

"I was always a very quiet child. I never associated much with other children. I never learned how to have friends. I was in and out of hospitals from age five to age eleven. The doctors didn't know what was wrong with me. They finally decided that it was a nervous condition and that the stress of school and public places was just too much for me to handle physically. So, my parents took me out of school for good and educated me at home. Soon, though, they realized that they didn't have time to take care of all my needs. They were California socialites and spent most of their time going to parties and social events. So, they hired tutors and nannies to take care of me. I actually got a very good education. I excelled in math and science. I was especially interested in brain chemistry," she continued. "I wanted to find out what made me different from other people. What in my brain caused me to get physically sick at the thought of public affairs and new people? I found that I had a severe case of agoraphobia.

"When I was twelve, my parents hired Mabel Walker. She was a twenty-five-year-old struggling actress. It was very difficult for her to find roles for a Negro woman, so she had to find another way to support herself. She would still go out and audition for plays and musicals in her spare time, though. I would even help her rehearse her lines for different parts. We became very close. She was the only friend I had and she stayed with me throughout my teenage years.

"When I was eighteen, my brother died of a drug overdose while at a party in Los Angeles. My parents didn't handle his death very well and decided that they wanted a completely different lifestyle. They needed to get away from the city. I couldn't imagine my life without Mabel so I begged her to come along. She didn't want to leave her dreams of becoming a star, but she saw how much I needed her, so she agreed to come with me for a little while.

"So, we moved here. My mother met Theodore's mother at a party and right away they began talking about their single, eligible children. Before I knew what was happening, I was obliged to go on a date with Theodore. I was so terrified. I hadn't met a new person in seven years and he was so much older than I was. I begged Mabel to come with me and she did.

"I think Theodore was very disappointed with me. He took us to this ridiculous play that I didn't understand. The more he tried to ask me questions and draw me out, the more I retreated into my shell. I didn't like him at all. He was too grand and boisterous and he treated me like I was a stupid little child. Thankfully, Mabel was there to divert his attention away from me. She was more on his level. They were both in their thirties and had similar interests. They spent the entire evening talking about art, music, and theater - - things I only knew about through Mabel.

"I was utterly shocked when he asked me out again. I didn't know what he was thinking. Once again, Mabel came along. After that, it was a regular event for the three of us to go out on the weekend. Most people thought that Mabel was the chaperone. I was so naive I couldn't even see that she was much more than that. I couldn't see that Theodore was in love with her. All I knew was that I didn't like him and I didn't want to keep seeing him, much less become his wife. I tried to tell my parents this, but they didn't care. They were just so excited that someone had shown an interest in me. And when he proposed, they were downright ecstatic. They had feared I would never land a husband.

"Before I knew it we were married. Mabel and I moved into the Phillips' mansion. He continued to treat me like a child. I finally started to notice how he was around

Mabel. He followed her around like an obsessed, lovesick puppy.

"What made it worse was that my parents had moved back to California. Now that I was married and out of their house, it was like a load had been lifted off their shoulders. I was completely alone. I was contemplating suicide when Matthew moved in. He was fifteen and the son of Theodore's college roommate, Titus Clare. Matthew's parents and his little brother, Stephen, had died in a house fire. Theodore was in the will as the guardian.

"Matthew was everything Theodore wasn't. He was kind, loving, thoughtful, and he treated me like a person. He would hear me crying at night and come hold me. We opened up to each other. I told him why I was unhappy and he revealed to me more about his family.

"Before long, Matthew and I fell in love and had an affair. Theodore didn't even notice. He was completely wrapped up in Mabel.

"When I found out I was pregnant, I knew it was Matthew's. I panicked and threw myself at Theodore so he would think the baby was his when it was born."

I heard everything she was saying, but it still hadn't sunk in. I wasn't even considering the identity of this baby. It was enough of a shock to learn that Matthew wasn't my brother and I couldn't even fathom the idea that he had slept with my mother.

185

"A couple of months later," she continued, "Mabel confided in me. She told me that she had never wanted a relationship with Theodore. She said she enjoyed working on music with him, but wanted nothing else. Theodore, however, wouldn't take 'no' for an answer and had forced himself on her and she was pregnant.

"I felt so guilty. I felt like I had put her in this position. She could still be in California, launching a successful movie career, if I hadn't convinced her to move with me. I hated Theodore even more. I wanted him out of our lives.

"When I gave birth, he didn't even come to the hospital to see me. Matthew was by my side the entire time. We named you after Matthew's little brother. When I got home, I decided that I'd had enough. I wanted him dead. I drew upon my knowledge of science and the brain to create a concoction that would give him an intracerebral aneurysm. The next morning, when I made him breakfast, I put it in his coffee. I couldn't watch him drink it so I went to my room, ashamed of what I had done. But I had to do it.

"When I came out, I saw that Theodore hadn't drunk the coffee, Mabel had. When she passed out due to the pressure on her brain, he took her to the hospital and she slipped into a coma. She hung on to life for three days, but when the aneurysm burst they knew she wouldn't make it, so they took the baby out and let Mabel die.

"I had killed my own best friend. I was so distraught that I told Matthew what I did. I had to get it off my chest. Theodore overheard and attacked me. He would have killed me if Matthew wasn't there. Theodore never forgave me for Mabel's death, and he has made me pay for it every day for eighteen years."

It was all coming together now. "Wait, Mother, are you saying that Matthew is my father?"

She kept going without answering my question directly. "The night Matthew…left, Theodore had come home unexpectedly and caught us in bed together. He shot Matthew in the shoulder and threatened to kill me if Matthew didn't leave forever. That's why Matthew left. When Theodore learned I was pregnant again, he knew it was Matthew's and he beat me until I lost the baby."

"Matthew never knew about you. Neither did Theodore. He never knew you were Matthew's child. I was just trying to protect you. I don't know what he would have done if he found out. He already hated you enough because you were my child."

"Matthew is my father." I kept repeating the phrase over and over.

"Yes," my mother answered, thinking it was a question. Really, I was just trying to convince myself.

"That means me and Ruthie aren't related!"

"You don't share a drop of blood."

I was so happy I felt like I could fly. I jumped up to run out to my truck, but then I remembered that I hadn't found out what happened here.

"Mother, where is Fath...where is he?"

"He's dead."

"What happened to him?" Just then I saw Matthew come in the back door with a shovel.

"Don't tell him anything. The less he knows, the safer he is." Matthew, my father, approached me and touched my face. "I'm so sorry, Stephen. I'm so sorry I wasn't there for you. I didn't know." He grabbed me and hugged me tight, like a father should. "I always wanted you to be mine."

I cried like I had never cried before. I wasn't crying out of despair and grief, the only kind of emotions I had known recently. I cried tears of joy and relief. I cried for a life of pain that was now in the past. I would never have to know that kind of pain again.

# Chapter 28

"Oh, my God," Lieutenant Drake said. "So all this time you and Ruthie weren't related at all?"

I shook my head.

"*Matthew* is your father?"

I nodded.

"It makes sense now. What you said earlier about there being no childhood pictures of Matthew. Why would there be? He wasn't there as a child." He leaned back in the chair and scratched his head. "Weren't you mad at your mother? You wasted two years of your life because you believed a lie."

I shrugged. "My mother has her own set of issues to deal with. I could never be angry with her."

Lieutenant Drake put his elbows on the table and massaged his temples with his fingers. "So where is she now? Where is your mother?" he asked.

"I don't know. After we cleaned up as best we could and explained everything to Ruthie, Matthew and my mother drove away in one direction, Ruthie and I in the other. I have no idea where they went or which one of them actually killed my father. It could have been both. I still wish it was me though. I wish I'd had the satisfaction of killing him."

Lt. Drake leaned back in his seat again and studied me. After a few moments he leaned forward again and said, "So let's say I believe you. Let's say you give me some leads on where I can find your...parents and I let you go. What do you plan on doing?"

I stared at him in disbelief. Was it possible he would just let Ruthie and me go? We wouldn't be tried as accomplices or anything? "I, um, well." I tried to hold back my excitement over the possibility. Ruthie and I made sure to not get too hopeful about our future. We had eluded the police for four, well, five days, but during that time we had feared the worst. Even though we hoped we could be together and overcome the trauma of our teenage years, we also knew we faced the possibility of jail time. We had just been involved in a murder.

"Well, um, the first chance I get I guess I'll marry Ruthie. After that...I don't know. I guess we'll just try to be happy. That's not an emotion we're used to."

I stared out the window so my face wouldn't betray my emotions. I didn't want him to see how desperate I was.

The sun was rising and the city was just waking up. I wondered if Ruthie was waking up, as well.

Lt. Drake sighed. "You hang tight. I'll be right back."

A few minutes later I heard the door of the interrogation room creak open. I kept looking out the window. I knew I would be able to tell with one look whether the lieutenant was going to let me go or not. I didn't want to turn around yet and face possible disappointment. But it wasn't Lieutenant Drake who had entered the room.

"Stephen?"

The sound of Ruthie's voice made my skin tingle. I leapt from the chair and folded her into my arms.

"Are you okay, Stephen?"

I nodded. Now that she was in my arms, I was more than okay.

"They're letting us go," she whispered in my ear.

I pulled away from our embrace and stared at her. "Are you serious?" I asked, wiping a tear from her eyes.

She nodded. "What did you tell them?"

I hugged her tightly again. "Shh," I whispered into her hair. "Don't say anything. The walls have ears."

Just then, the door swung open. Lieutenant Drake and the fat, smelly officer that had begun the interview nine hours ago entered. My arm tightened around Ruthie's waist as I remembered how he called her a nigger.

"You two are free to go," Lieutenant Drake said. The other officer let out a sigh and rolled his eyes. "Tom, we already discussed this. It's my call."

"And it's the wrong call," Tom said. "I don't buy it. I just don't buy it. They know more." He stared at us as if he could see through us and into our souls. I wanted to get out of that room as soon as possible, but for some reason I felt frozen in place. I couldn't move. I continued my staring match with the officer named Tom until Ruthie nudged me in the back. Finally, I put one foot in front of the other and with Ruthie's hand in mine, I walked toward the door.

Tom didn't move as we approached him. He kept staring at us as Ruthie squeezed past his big belly. When we were finally past him and in the hallway, Lieutenant Drake called my name.

"You kids take care," he said handing me a business card. "If there's anything I can do for you, let me know."

I slid the card in my back pocket. I probably should have said thank you or something, but it slipped my mind. All I could think about was getting out of that police station and starting my new life with Ruthie. I led her to the parking lot where we found my pickup truck. I opened her door for her, then ran around to the other side.

After I slid into the driver's seat we both sat in stunned silence for a moment.

Finally, I started the car and pulled out of the parking space.

"I can't believe they're letting us go," Ruthie said a few minutes later as we pulled onto the interstate. "I can't believe they bought that story."

"Every word." I leaned over and kissed her.

"So, we're off the hook? They're gonna leave us alone for good?"

I grabbed her hand and squeezed.

"What do you say we go get married or something?"

Ruthie smiled broadly. "Let's do it."

"We have to hurry up and get out of town first. It's only going to take a couple of hours before they realize Matthew never existed."

# Epilogue

A lot of what I told Lieutenant Drake was true. My father was abusive, my mother was a basket case, and I've been in love with Ruthie for as long as I can remember. But that's about it. I never had a dog; I'm allergic. I slipped up and told Lieutenant Drake that I was allergic to pets, but thankfully, he didn't catch it. More importantly, though, I never had a brother. What I do have is a sister, Ruthie.

People like Matthew just don't exist. Someone that inherently good? That kind of sunshine couldn't possibly be real. I was surprised I could even dream him up in my mind. Thankfully, I had Ruthie and her imagination to help me.

Julius was real. He was my only friend besides Ruthie and he was there when I needed him. He's also the person who planted the seed of an idea that I should just run away with Ruthie. It took two years for that seed to take root in my mind, but after it did, there was nothing that would stop me from making it happen. Especially not my father.

I honestly have no idea about my mother's past. I guess what I said about her life is possible, but I really have no idea. She would never share something like that with me.

My mother has never spoken more than ten words at a time to me in her entire life. Ruthie and I argued for hours about my mother's part of the story. I thought it sounded ridiculous that neither of us would notice she was the same age as Matthew. But in the end she convinced me that adults underestimate children all the time. She was right. Lieutenant Drake never even questioned that part of the story.

For two years I blamed myself and lived in shame for the inappropriate feelings I had for my half sister. But when she came back for Adelaide's wedding, all that shame vanished. I didn't care anymore. I had to have her. It wasn't fair that we could never be happy just because of circumstances that occurred before we were even born.

At the wedding reception Julius once again told me I should just run away with Ruthie. "Don't think about the half that's related," he said. "Concentrate on the half that ain't." His advice stuck. I whispered his words to Ruthie as we held each other on that dance floor. That's when we decided we had to be together no matter what.

I only intended to go home for a second. I thought maybe I could convince my mother to come with us. I didn't want to leave her alone with him. But if she refused, I wasn't going to let that stop me. I would say goodbye to my mother and move on with my life.

Five minutes would have made all the difference. Ruthie and I would have been gone before my father arrived and we would never be seen again. But as it happened, just when we stepped off the front porch to head to my truck, my father's white Cadillac pulled up.

He blocked my truck with his car and hopped out. "Where do you think you're going with my daughter?" he said, approaching me. Ruthie clutched my shirt and hid behind me.

"Get in the truck, Ruthie," I said, gently pushing her. Slowly she inched away.

I wasn't afraid or angry. Amazingly, I was completely calm. Like his behavior had no effect on me. I was determined to be with Ruthie.

"You can't do this," he said. "This is disgusting. It's an abomination."

"You're the abomination," I said.

He had raised his hand to strike me when I heard a sudden "thunk." He froze. His eyes went blank and he collapsed to the ground.

I looked up and saw Ruthie standing over my father, our father, with a shovel.

My mother, who was standing behind me on the porch, started screaming wildly.

"Oh my God. Oh my God. Oh my God." Ruthie dropped the shovel and covered her mouth.

I stepped over my father's body and gathered her in my arms. "Shh. It's okay. Shh."

197

"I'm so sorry. I just couldn't stand to see him hurt you again. What have I done? I didn't mean to kill him," she said, burying her face into my chest.

He wasn't dead. I saw his eyes blink as blood started to drip from his lips.

"Go inside. Take my mother inside the house," I told Ruthie.

"Oh my God, Stephen. What did I do?"

"Shh. Just go inside. I'll take care of this."

Ruthie obeyed and tried to guide my now-hysterical mother inside the house.

I stayed outside and stared at my father's bloodied face. His life was slowly drifting out of him. I picked up the shovel and finished what Ruthie had started.

My mother never did calm down. She would never be the same. We loaded her in the car and drove her to a mental institution in West Virginia. Then Ruthie and I kept driving. On the way, we concocted the story about Matthew just in case we were caught. A simple busted tail light is what landed us in that police station in Chicago. And once they found out who I was, I was arrested and the interrogation began.

I'm still amazed they believed me. I slipped up a couple of times. I told the lieutenant I didn't drink coffee, but then I told him I drank coffee the morning Ruthie went to New York. It was an elaborate lie and some things were hard to keep straight. But overall, I did pretty well. I'm a very convincing person, which is why Ruthie and I decided I should do the talking. No one would believe her. Not because she's black but because she's too sweet. She feels too much. It's part of the reason why I love her so. She makes me feel as well. She melted away the numbing emptiness that my life had become.

It's all over now. The truth didn't set us free. My lies did.

Once a year, Ruthie and I carefully plan a trip to visit my mother. Sometimes she recognizes us and sometimes she doesn't. Sometimes she won't even talk to us because she thinks we're Theodore and Mabel.

Ruthie and I have a relatively normal life living in Canada, just across Michigan's border. She's sold several paintings under her assumed name, Saffron James. I work in a bottling factory during the day and take college classes at night.

We're careful. We don't talk about Virginia. We don't call each other by our real names, even when we're alone. I think we both secretly pretend that Matthew Clare really is my father. It helps us both sleep better at night. With each passing day, the guilt subsides a little more.

No one suspects. No one will ever know. Because she's black and I'm white, no one looks close enough to realize we have the same shaped chin and ears. To everyone else, we're just a young couple in love.

# About the Author

Leslie DuBois lives in Charleston, South Carolina with her husband and two children. She currently attends the Medical University where she's earning her PhD in Biostatistics. Leslie enjoys writing stories and novels that integrate races. Her other novels include Guardian of Eden, The Queen Bee of Bridgeton and La Cienega Just Smiled coming November 2011. She also writes as Sybil Nelson. Visit her at www.LeslieDuBois.com to learn more.

# Reading Group Guide

1. Why did Stephen choose to begin his story when he was five-years-old in 1963? Would the story have been as effective if set in modern times? What would have needed to change? How would modern day technology affect Stephen's story?

2. What part did race play in the development of Stephen and Ruthie's love? Would they have felt as strongly about each other if they were the same race? Would they have suspected their true relationship if they were the same race? How would things have been different if Stephen and Ruthie learned the truth earlier?

3. Why was Matthew a necessary character in Stephen's story? How did Matthew's character help garner sympathy for Stephen and Ruthie in the eyes of the Lieutenant? Did anything about Matthew's character at the beginning of the book seem unlikely?

4. We briefly meet a racist officer named Tom, did Tom's prejudice help Stephen's credibility from the point of view of Lt. Drake?

5. How did the mental states of Marjorie and Grandma Esther play a role in Stephen's story? Would his tale have been as effective if they were both mentally competent? Why or why not?

6. How did segregation and racism affect Theodore's life and decisions? Was Theodore free to make his own choices about whom to love? Did he really love Ruthie and her mother? Why didn't he confess sooner?

7. Why was Julius important to the plot? Would things have been different without him, or would Stephen eventually have come to the same conclusion to "concentrate on the half that ain't?"

8. Why did Stephen and Marjorie stay in an abusive home for so long? Can what Stephen and Ruthie did be called "Self-defense?" Why or why not? If it is self-defense, why not just tell Lt. Drake the truth? Would Lt. Drake have been as sympathetic?

9. What inconsistencies did you find in Stephen's story, or were you completely fooled? If so, why? What questions are you left with after Stephen's revelation about Matthew? Was Stephen really abused by his father? Or are he and Ruthie just psychopaths?

10. In your opinion, who really is the "abomination?" Theodore or Stephen?

# A Sneak Peek into Guardian of Eden by Leslie DuBois

## Prologue:

## Man vs. Evil

"Somebody help, please!"

A man in blue scrubs rushed toward me, took my sister's limp body from my arms and placed her on a gurney. He flashed a light in her eyes and took her pulse as a woman fired questions at me.

"Are you her boyfriend?"

"Boyfriend? She's 12!"

"How long has she been unconscious?"

"She passed out in the car. About 10 minutes. She said her stomach hurts." My voice, usually deeper than most teenage boys', sounded shrill, and broken, almost child-like as it resonated against the cold sterile walls of the near-empty emergency room.

"Is she on drugs?"

"Drugs? She's only 12!" The man and woman wheeled my sister into a room. I tried to follow, but another woman pulled me aside and started examining me, probing me with both her questions and her hands. "What are you doing?" I asked when she lifted up my shirt.

"Where were you stabbed?"

"Stabbed?"

"Yes, I'm trying to find the source of the blood."

"Blood?" I looked down and gasped at the bright-red stain soaking my shirt and my pants from mid chest all the way to my knees. Trapped in the urgency of the moment, I hadn't noticed the wetness of my clothing. Now that the adrenaline started to wear off, it came into focus. My shirt stuck to my skin where my sister's blood started drying. "Oh my God," I said, allowing my weight to shift towards the wall as I felt my knees weaken. I misjudged the distance and stumbled.

"I think he's going into shock," she yelled, trying to steady me with her gloved hands. "We need another gurney!"

"No, no, I'm fine. Just help Eden, please."

"Are you sure?"

"Yes, the blood's not mine. It's hers."

Her eyes bulged she stepped back and looked at the amount of blood on me. "Dr. Shepherd we need you in number one," she shouted as she whirled away in a blur of white. "The girl's hemorrhaging!" The nurse charged behind the curtain with an IV pole, a bag of fluid, and a fistful of test tubes. I heard her bark orders from behind the ugly blue fabric. "We need stat labs. I think she's going to need refill."

Out of the corner of my eye, I saw Maddie enter the emergency room and run to me. "What did they say? What's wrong with her?" she said. I shrugged and placed my head in my hands. Maddie sat down next to me and rubbed my back. "Don't worry, Garrett. She'll be fine."

I shook my head to fight back the tears. Too many had fallen in my lifetime. At seventeen, I was already tired of crying.

"Garrett, she's strong. She's tougher than you give her credit for. Both of you have had to be to make it this far. You'll make it through this too."Maddie weaved her fingers in mine and lifted my hand to her lips. She tried to comfort me, but her words felt empty and meaningless in my despair. She didn't understand. Yes, Eden and I had been through a lot of turmoil and survived. I knew how to shield her from all our previous trials. But how do I protect her from what I

206

don't know? She was already sick. Obviously, danger had seeped in and I wasn't there to prevent it. I didn't protect her.

Maddie continued to hold my hand as she started chewing on her bottom lip and tapping her foot. Moments later she let go of my hand, jumped out of her seat then paced the floor while mindlessly snapping her fingers. After about thirty seconds, she sat back down, took my hand, and rested her head on my shoulder as if she might fall asleep. In an instant, she was up again and pacing. Suddenly, she stopped and stared at me.

"We should get you out of those clothes. I'll go see what's in the car," she said as she dashed out of the door to the parking lot. She needed to do something to occupy her time and keep her mind off of Eden.

After she left, I walked up to the reception area and said, "Excuse me, but I brought in the little girl a few minutes ago. Can you tell me anything yet? Is she conscious?"

The short brunette shook her head apologetically. "As soon as I find out something, I'll let you know. You can help things along by filling this out, though." She handed me a clipboard with some papers.

As soon as I sat down, Maddie returned. She handed me a T-shirt. "This was all I could find." She sat down next to me and resumed her nervous habits.

I spent the next fifteen minutes filling out forms. I didn't think to bring Eden's insurance card so I had to recall the information from memory. Usually, I have a perfect photographic memory, but when I'm stressed, it fails. It took several tries before I could see the numbers on her card in my head. I also wrote down everything I knew about Eden's medical history. There wasn't much. Of the two of us, she was always healthier. The only time she had ever been to a hospital was to visit me. When I finished, I went to the bathroom and cleaned up.

\*\*\*

"Who is responsible for this girl?" The doctor demanded as he stormed into the waiting room.

"I am," I said, standing up so quickly I woke Maddie who had fallen asleep on my shoulder.

"And just who are you?"

"I'm her brother." The doctor raised his left eyebrow and looked me up and down. I knew exactly what he was thinking. "Look, we have the same mother, but my father is black, her father is white. Now can you tell me what's wrong with her?"

"Brother, huh? I think it's time to get the police involved." The doctor turned his back to me and stepped toward the nurse's station.

"Police? What the...?" I reached out and grabbed his shoulder.

I just wanted him to explain, but the doctor reacted to the motion as a sign of aggression and yelled, "Security!"

"Wait, wait, wait," Maddie said, taking my hand and stepping between me and the doctor. "He didn't mean anything. He just really needs to know what's going on. My boyfriend is very protective of his little sister."

The doctor studied the two of us for a few seconds. He must have instantly trusted Maddie's big blue eyes. Everyone did. Including me. She had an innocence, an honesty, in her sweet round face that melted away doubt and suspicion.

"Let me see some identification from both of you." I took out my wallet and handed him my student I.D. while Maddie fumbled around in her purse. She couldn't find her wallet. She dumped the contents of her bag onto the floor and searched on hands and knees.

"Damn it. I left my wallet," she mumbled as she turned red. Then she whipped off her necklace and stood. "This has my medical information," she told the doctor holding the necklace in front of him. "There's my name and my address and my father's name if you want to call him."

"Bartholomew McPhee?" the doctor asked. "Senator Bartholomew McPhee is your father?" She nodded. He looked from Maddie to me then back. He knew he needed to proceed cautiously in dealing with the daughter of a Virginia senator, especially when that senator currently occupied all the news headlines. He cleared his throat then waved off the security guard. "Do you have any contact information for your mother?" he asked, trying not to seem uneasy about Maddie's parentage.

"She's visiting her mother in North Carolina this weekend." I wrote my mother's cell phone number on his clipboard.

"Eden's in exam room 3," he called over his shoulder as he stormed off to the nurse's station and picked up the phone. Before dialing he added, "If you upset her in anyway, I'm banning you from her room."

Eden started crying and held her arms out to me when I entered her room.

"What's wrong with me, Gary? Am I dying? It hurts so bad." I crawled into bed next to her and held her just like I did when she was little. Cramming ourselves into a small bed didn't bother either one of us. We had slept in worse conditions.

"Shhh. Don't cry. You're not dying. I would never let that happen. The doctors here are going to fix you up and you're gonna be just fine." I stroked her dark blonde hair and stared into her brown-green eyes.

"You promise?"

"I promise. I would never let anything bad happen to you." Eden cried harder. She cried herself into exhaustion and fell asleep in my arms.

\*\*\*

"I brought you some coffee," Maddie whispered as she entered the room. I hadn't even noticed she left.

"You don't have to whisper. She's sound asleep. Eden could sleep through a tornado." I slid out of the hospital bed then took the cup of coffee she held out to me.

"Is she okay?"

I nodded as I took a sip. It tasted wretched. I put the lid back on and placed it on the table.

Maddie hugged herself and stared down at my little sister. She was worried about her. Over the past few months, she'd grown quite attached to Eden. I stepped behind her, put my hands on her shoulders and kissed the top of her platinum blonde head.

"You called me your boyfriend. You've never called me your boyfriend before." Maddie turned around and stared up at me with her blue-lake eyes. Eyes so wide and blue and soft I wanted to drown in them. She stood up straight and wrapped her arms around my neck. She almost couldn't reach even on her tiptoes. At sixteen years old, Maddie was two inches shorter than my twelve-year-old sister. But then again Eden was taller than most twelve-year-olds, a great asset in her modeling career.

Maddie ran her fingers through my long black hair and as tears welled in her eyes she said, "I love you, Garrett."

"I love you, too," I said before pressing my lips to hers. It should have the happiest moment in my life. Madison McPhee loved me. But I couldn't fully enjoy it knowing my sister was suffering just feet away.

"What about your father? What about the election?" I asked after kissing her breathless.

"I don't care what he says. I need you, I want you, and I can't exist without you." We both smiled as she repeated the exact same words I'd told her just two weeks ago.

"Now you're just picking on me," I said.

"Well, you have to admit, it's a pretty corny line."

"It wasn't a line. It's the truth." I kissed her again. Our kiss deepened as I pulled her closer to me. I don't know what would have happened if we weren't interrupted by a soft tapping on the door.

"May we speak to you in the hall?" the doctor asked me after poking his head in. "I'm sorry I didn't introduce myself properly," he said once we left the room. "I'm Dr. Shepherd and this is Rowena Smith from Child Services."

I shook both their hands and said, "I don't understand why Child Services is here?" while eyeing them suspiciously. I'd seen enough of Child Services for five lifetimes.

"We spoke to your mother," Dr. Shepherd said ignoring my question. "She faxed over a letter giving you power of attorney over Eden. She trusts you to make all the decisions concerning her welfare." That letter was worthless in my book. I'd already been doing that for the past twelve years.

"Will you tell me what's wrong with my sister, please?" Dr. Shepherd and Rowena Smith exchanged a look, a look of foreboding that instantly made my heart race.

"You might want to sit down, son," the overweight black lady said as she put her hand on my shoulder."

"I don't want to sit down. I want to know what's wrong with her."

Dr. Shepherd sighed and said, "Your sister had a miscarriage." I stared at him blankly as the words swirled around my mind. Everything logical in me told me it was impossible.

"I'm sorry. You must be looking at the wrong chart. My sister is only twelve."

"It's not a mistake, Garrett. We've already performed the D&C. The fetus was about 6 weeks old." My knees gave out. I collapsed in a chair. My heart tightened in my chest. My stomach revolted. I thought I might vomit. The doctor kept talking, but I really couldn't hear anything else.

"Who did this? Who could do that to a child?" I asked, interrupting the doctor's details.

"We need your help to figure that out," Rowena said. "Does she have a boyfriend? Is there any chance this was consensual?"

I glared at her. How could she even suggest something like that?

"A detective is on the way," she said once she noticed my fierce expression. "Do you know anything that may help with the investigation?"

I shook my head. I knew nothing. What kind of brother was I to let something like this happen? I should have been paying more attention to her. This was my fault and I was going to fix it.

*** 

Eden began to stir around five o'clock in the morning. I asked Maddie to leave the room for a few minutes. Eden cried for me and I took her hand.

"Eden, I know something bad happened to you," I said as I tucked her hair behind her ear. "I know I let you down."

"Gary, don't cry. It's not your fault." She reached up and wiped a tear from my face.

"Tell me what happened. Tell me who hurt you."

\*\*\*

"Give me your keys," I said to Maddie twenty minutes later.

"Why? Where are you going?" I didn't respond. "Garrett, what's wrong? Is it about Eden?" Her eyes were filled with fear as I towered over her. Maddie handed me her keys and I left the hospital without saying another word.

\*\*\*

I remember picking up the gun and loading it. I even remember pointing it at his head. I remember thinking that I was ruining my life and probably Maddie's as well. I remember the overwhelming need to rid Eden of this evil in her life. What I don't remember is pulling the trigger and pulling it six times.

Made in the USA
Charleston, SC
26 October 2011